Science Concepts SECOND SERIES

Energy

Alvin Silverstein, Virginia Silverstein, and Laura Silverstein Nunn

Twenty-First Century Books
Minneapolis

Twenty-First Century Books
A division of Lerner Publishing Group, Inc.
241 First Avenue North
Minneapolis, MN 55401 U.S.A.

Website address: www.lernerbooks.com

Library of Congress Cataloging-in-Publication Data

Silverstein, Alvin.
     Energy / by Alvin Silverstein, Virginia Silverstein, Laura Silverstein Nunn. —
Rev. ed.
        p.   cm. — (Science concepts : second series)
  Includes bibliographical references and index.
     ISBN 978–0–8225–8655–5 (lib. bdg. : alk. paper)
     1. Power resources—Juvenile literature. I. Silverstein, Virginia B. II. Nunn,
Laura Silverstein. III. Title.
  TJ163.23.S555 2009
  621.042—dc22   2007049535

Manufactured in the United States of America
1 2 3 4 5 6 – DP – 14 13 12 11 10 09

Contents

chapter one

Energy for Life

How do you feel when the power goes out in your

neighborhood? You can't turn on a light. You can't

watch television, check your e-mail, or play video

games. You can't even cook food. If you feel helpless,

you're not alone.

We depend so much on electricity that living without it would be not only inconvenient but dangerous. Without air conditioners during sizzling-hot summers, some people might die from heat stroke. During bitter-cold winters, some people rely on electric heaters. Even furnaces fueled by oil or natural gas cannot run without electricity. Electricity powers thermostats that turn heaters and furnaces on and off. Traffic lights, elevators, telephones, computers—all run on electricity. But what is electricity? Electricity is a form of energy.

All living things need energy to live. The Sun sends a continuous stream of light energy to Earth. Plants turn sunlight energy into energy-rich chemical compounds that they store as food. Plant-eating animals use some of the chemicals in the plants to maintain their own life processes. In turn, other animals eat the plant-eating animals to gain the energy-rich chemicals they need to live. Sunlight

The food cycle is the connection between all living things. Energy from the Sun nourishes plants, which are eaten by animals. Other animals eat these animals. All of these animals provide increased nourishment for plants as the animals break down after they die.

energy also provides the heat that living things on our planet need to survive.

Early humans discovered another powerful source of energy—fire. Among its many uses, fire provides warmth, cooks food, gives light, and helps in making tools. The discovery of fire dramatically changed people's lifestyles. We still depend on fire in the twenty-first century. For example, a gas stove's burners cook food, the fire in a furnace supplies heat to the radiators that keep our houses warm, and the engines in our cars burn gasoline to power the turning wheels.

What Is Energy?

How do you use the word *energy*? You might say, "Boy, I have a lot of energy today. I feel like I can run for hours." Or you might think, "I'm feeling pretty tired. I must be a little low on energy." But you might also use the word *energy* when you talk about electric power or natural resources such as fossil fuels—coal, gas, and oil. Fossil fuels come from the remains of ancient plants and animals and are one of the main sources of energy for modern machines.

When scientists talk about energy, they are referring to the capacity to do work—to move an object or to bring about a change in the state of matter. Matter is anything that has a definite amount of substance, or mass, and takes up space. A blade of grass, a stone, a child, an ocean, and a planet are all examples of matter. So is the air in our atmosphere, even though we cannot see it. Matter can exist in three main states: solid (such as a stone or grass), liquid (such as milk or seawater), and gas (such as air).

When work is performed, energy is used to overcome some resistance to movement. Gravity, for instance, is a force that pulls matter toward Earth's surface. When you try to lift a heavy desk, it's really hard because gravity is pulling the desk downward. (The effects of gravity are felt in the form of weight.) So you have to use energy to do the work of lifting the desk.

Did You Know?

Energy comes from a Greek word that means "work."

Left: *Milk, a liquid, is poured into a glass, a solid.* Right: *When this girl breathes outside on a cold night, she can see her breath in the air, a gas.*

The Many Forms of Energy

Energy exists in two states—potential and kinetic. Potential energy is stored energy that has the potential—the future ability—to perform work. A boulder that sits on top of a hill is not actively doing work but has the capacity to do so because of its position. When gravity causes the boulder to roll down the hill, the boulder's potential energy turns into kinetic energy.

Kinetic energy, the energy of motion, is the form of energy that actively performs work. Kinetic energy can be converted (changed) into potential energy too. Pushing the boulder up the hill involves kinetic energy, which then becomes potential energy when the boulder is back on top of the hill.

Kinetic and potential energy can exist in many different forms. Kinetic energy may include:

- Light energy, involving the movement of photons (units of light energy)

- Heat energy, involving the movement of atoms (the smallest particles of matter)
- Mechanical energy, pertaining to the movement of machine parts
- Electrical energy, involving the movement of electrically charged particles
- Magnetism, associated with electricity, and involving an attraction to objects made of iron (for example, a magnetic compass)
- Gravitational energy, involving the force of attraction between two objects of matter

This antique compass uses the magnetism of Earth to tell the user what direction he or she is facing.

Potential energy can include all these kinds of energy and some others as well, for example:

- Chemical energy, which is stored in the bonds that hold atoms together in molecules. The stored, or potential, energy is turned into a kinetic energy when these bonds are broken and a chemical reaction occurs. The digestion of food and the explosion of a stick of dynamite are both examples of this kind of energy conversion.
- Nuclear energy, which is stored within atoms. When the structure of atoms is changed, a nuclear reaction may occur, such as in the atomic bombs used against Japan to end World War II (1939–1945). In a nuclear reaction, some of the matter in the atoms is actually converted to energy.

One form of energy can be converted into other forms. For instance, electrical energy changes into heat to operate a toaster, into sound to make a telephone work, and into light to make a lightbulb glow. Heat energy is turned into mechanical energy to make a car's engine perform.

Lifting your hand to turn the pages of a book involves the conversion of chemical to electrical energy. Your brain uses the energy from food chemicals to produce electrical signals that tell the muscles in your hand what to do. Chemical energy is also converted to mechanical energy, working your muscles to move your hand against the resistance of gravity.

Energy in the Modern World

As the human population has continued to grow and as humans continue to invent new products, the demand for energy has increased. And yet, our natural resources are limited. For example, the fossil fuels we rely on in the twenty-first century—to fuel cars and airplanes, to heat our homes, and to power our computers—were formed millions of years ago, under conditions that no longer exist on Earth. Once we use up all the coal, oil, and natural gas that lies deep underground, there will be no more.

How long will the world's supplies of fossil fuels last? The experts are debating that question. Some say we have enough to cover our needs for another century or two. Others think we may run out of oil, gas, and coal within fifty years or less.

Depending too much on fossil fuels creates other problems, as well. For example, burning fossil fuels to generate energy produces harmful chemicals that are polluting our air, water, and soil. One of these products is a gas called carbon dioxide. This gas is entering Earth's atmosphere in increasing amounts. It holds in some of the heat from sunlight and gradually adds to the warming of our planet. That temperature rise could bring major changes in our environment, our lives, and the lives of all Earth's creatures. For example, we are beginning to see a rise in the severity of storms such as hurricanes and tornadoes. The huge ice sheets at the North Pole and the South Pole are beginning to melt, and the ocean waters are getting warmer. As a result, the level of the ocean is rising. Eventually, some of the world's major cities may be flooded.

For all these reasons, people are searching for alternative energy sources that do not depend on our limited supplies of fossil fuels. The new energy sources must also be "clean" energy, producing no chemicals that would harm the environment. They include power from wind and water, sunlight energy, and heat energy from deep underground. Researchers are even working out ways to get energy from trash and animal wastes.

People all over the world are "going green"—finding ways to use less energy and produce less pollution. For example, turning off lights when you leave a room and turning off your computer when you aren't using it can save energy. Recycling newspapers, aluminum cans, and plastic bottles can help reduce waste. Riding a bike or walking to a friend's house instead of having your parents drive you not only saves fossil fuels but also helps keep you fit. With these new approaches, we can keep our planet green and healthy.

chapter two

Electrical Energy

Ancient people did not know that electricity exists. In fact, lightning was one of nature's great mysteries. The ancient Greeks thought that angry gods were hurling thunderbolts from the heavens. In some African societies, places and people that were struck by lightning were believed to be cursed.

The first experiments on electricity took place more than two thousand years ago. About 600 B.C., the Greek scientist Thales of Miletus rubbed a yellow substance called amber (tree sap that turned solid) with a piece of wool or fur. He brought it near a light object, such as a feather. An immediate attraction occurred between the feather and the amber—the feather flew up and clung to the amber. Thales could not explain this "strange property" of amber. He thought the amber was alive and lured nonliving material to itself, almost as though it was breathing and sucking in air.

In 1570 William Gilbert, doctor to Queen Elizabeth I of England, showed that other materials such as glass, sulfur, and sealing wax, had properties similar to that of amber. Gilbert called these amazing properties "electrics" from the word *electron*, which is Greek for amber. In 1646 Sir Thomas Browne, an English doctor, was the first to use the word *electricity*.

In 1752 Benjamin Franklin carried out his famous lightning experiment in Philadelphia, Pennsylvania. Franklin tied a metal key to the end of a homemade kite and flew it during a thunderstorm. When a bolt of lightning struck his kite, it traveled down the wet kite string to the key and created a spark. Franklin proved that lightning is actually a form of electricity. This experiment was very dangerous. Franklin could feel the electric spark on his knuckles, which were next to the key. Two other scientists tried to duplicate Franklin's kite experiment and died.

This illustration from the late 1800s shows Benjamin Franklin (right) *and his son William doing an experiment using a kite and a metal key to prove that lightning is a form of electricity.*

What Is Electricity?

When materials such as amber, glass, and plastic are rubbed, they become electrically charged. But what does that mean? To understand how objects get an electric charge, we need to look at the source—atoms.

Everything around us is made up of atoms. Atoms are tiny individual particles found in matter. A single atom is a million times smaller than the thickness of a human hair. Atoms are the building blocks of the simplest substances, called chemical elements, which include hydrogen, oxygen, iron, and lead.

Atoms often join together with other atoms to form molecules. Each kind of molecule has a different arrangement of atoms. The unique grouping of atoms of two or more different elements (in a molecule) is called a compound. For example, water is a compound in which each molecule consists of two atoms of hydrogen linked to one atom of oxygen. Its chemical formula is written as H_2O.

Atoms are made up of three kinds of particles—protons, neutrons, and electrons. Protons and neutrons are located in the center of the atom, called the nucleus. Protons carry a positive charge and neutrons have no charge (that is, they are electrically neutral). Electrons have a negative charge. They revolve through an empty space outside the atom's nucleus and travel at amazing speeds.

Normally, the number of protons in an atom is the same as the number of electrons. Therefore, their charges cancel each other out. The atom as a whole remains electrically neutral. But an atom can gain or lose electrons in a chemical reaction. If an atom gains some electrons, it becomes negatively charged. If an atom loses some electrons, it becomes positively charged. Atoms that have an electric charge—either positive or negative—are called ions. Electricity is simply the movement of electrons.

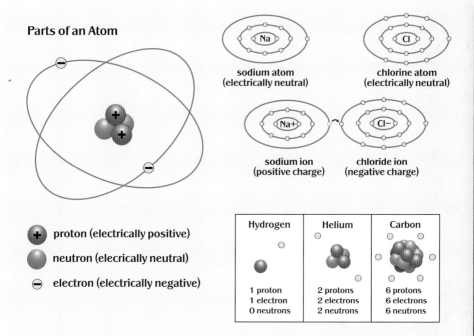

Atoms have three parts: protons, neutrons, and electrons. Protons and neutrons are at the center of the atom, and electrons move in the space around them. When an atom loses or gains electrons, it becomes electrically charged and is called an ion. The diagram on the top right shows ions forming. The box shows the atoms of some common elements.

Basic Law of Electricity

In 1733 French scientist Charles Du Fay made a fascinating discovery. When he rubbed two amber beads, each dangling from a separate string, they repelled (pushed away from) each other and moved apart. But then he replaced one of the amber beads with a glass bead and rubbed them. They moved together and clung to each other, as though they were attracted by some invisible force.

Du Fay realized that there must be two kinds of electrical charges, positive and negative. He then formed a basic law of electricity: Like charges repel, and unlike charges attract. Therefore, two positive charges repel each other; and two negative charges also repel each other. But a positive charge and a negative charge attract each other. This law is essential to understanding electricity.

The space around a charged particle, in which its charge produces an effect, is called an electric field. The electric field causes charged particles to create a force against one another, even when they are not physically touching. Ions with opposite charges are attracted to one another. Those with the same kind of charge repel (push away from) one another. For example, when Thales rubbed a piece of wool against amber, some of the electrons from the wool transferred to the amber. The amber became negatively charged, and an electric field formed.

When Thales brought a feather into the electric field, it became attracted to the amber. The feather originally had no electric charge. But the extra electrons in the negatively charged amber repelled some of the electrons in the feather. The electrons in the feather moved as far away as they could. The feather ended up with a positive charge on the side closest to the amber and a negative charge on the side away from it.

Forms of Electricity

Electricity occurs in two forms: static and current. Static electricity is simply electric charges at rest—that is, electrons or ions that do not move. Have you ever combed your hair, especially on a dry day, and found the strands of hair crackling and standing straight up? This happens because of static electricity.

This girl has her hands on a static electricity generator. The static electricity causes her hair to stand up.

When a comb goes through your hair, the hair loses electrons and becomes positively charged. So the positively charged hairs repel one another. The comb gains electrons, becoming negatively charged. Have you ever walked across a carpet, then touched a metal object, such as a doorknob, and felt a mild shock? Static electricity again. And, of course, the same thing happened with Thales's amber.

Current electricity consists of moving electrons or ions. Normally, electrons and ions move randomly. However, if two points have different amounts of stored electrical energy (for example, an electrical outlet and a lamp), charged particles will move continuously through the substance connecting them (that is, the lamp's electrical cord). The charged particles all move in the same direction, producing an electric current. The path along which current electricity flows is called a circuit.

Materials that carry electricity from one place to another are called conductors. Some materials, including metals such as copper, aluminum, and silver, are better conductors than others. To conduct electricity, a substance must contain charged particles that are free to move. In a metal wire, some of the electrons are bound loosely to their atoms, so they are able to move from one atom to another.

In some materials, such as glass, plastic, and rubber, the electrons are bound so tightly to their atoms that few can move freely. These materials, known as insulators, are not able to conduct electricity.

Metal, such as this copper wire (left)*, conducts electricity well. Rubber, such as this airplane tire* (right)*, does not conduct electricity.*

Electricity Gets Practical

In 1780 Italian anatomy professor Luigi Galvani was dissecting a frog in a laboratory also used for electrical experiments. While Galvani was poking at the frog's legs with a steel scalpel, a nearby static electricity machine made a spark. Suddenly, the frog's legs twitched.

In another experiment, Galvani hung legs of some freshly killed frogs on a brass hook over an iron fence. When the legs touched the fence, the muscles twitched and pulled away from the iron. Galvani realized that electric currents made the muscles move. This happened only when the frogs' legs connected the two kinds of metal. But Galvani could not figure out how the electricity was created. He thought that the frog was the source of the electricity and wrongly named his discovery "animal electricity."

Italian physics professor Alessandro Volta figured out what was actually happening in Galvani's experiment. The moisture in the frog legs provided a connection that let electrons flow between the iron and the brass. This electric current made the leg muscles twitch.

In an experiment in 1800, Volta produced a powerful source of electric current. He set up alternating strips of zinc and silver. He separated them with pieces of cardboard soaked in salt water. A chemical reaction took place in the metallic zinc, which lost electrons to form positively charged zinc ions.

Electrons flowed from the zinc to the silver, through the saltwater "bridge." This was the first

If the two wires of this voltaic battery are brought into contact, electrons flow from the zinc discs toward the silver discs.

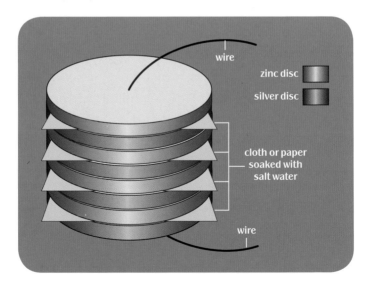

wire

zinc disc

silver disc

cloth or paper soaked with salt water

wire

battery, known as the voltaic pile (named after Volta). The two pieces of metal in the battery are called electrodes. The one that produces electrons (zinc in this case) has a negative charge and is called the cathode. The electrode that receives electrons (silver in Volta's battery) has a positive charge and is called the anode.

Volta's battery was the world's first steady supply of electricity. Before the battery, only static electricity could be produced and electricity was no more than an intriguing curiosity. But finally, electricity had some practical use. It could be stored and then released as needed.

The batteries (dry cells) used in flashlights and toys work on the same basic principle as Volta's invention. They are very

All of these batteries are dry cells. They provide the electricity that runs many of the portable devices people use every day.

inefficient, though. The power they produce is only 2 percent of the energy that was used to make them. Also, they stop working when their chemicals are used up. The lead-acid batteries used in cars and trucks last much longer because they are constantly recharged as the vehicle runs. Nickel-cadmium (NiCad) or "rechargeable" batteries look like the disposable kind, but they can be recharged in special devices that plug into the household current.

Electric cars run on energy stored in batteries. They are slower than conventional cars, powered by internal combustion engines (that is, engines that burn gasoline). They are also less convenient because they have to stop often for recharging. But they are much cleaner and more energy efficient than cars that burn gasoline or other fuels that send poisonous fumes into the air. They are useful mainly in cities, where high speed and long distances are less important than keeping pollution from creating a serious health problem.

Starting in 2000, hybrid cars began to grow in popularity. Hybrid cars can switch between gasoline combustion and stored electricity as the power source. They combine the advantages of both types of cars. They can be used for all kinds of driving but create less pollution than gasoline-fueled cars.

The fuel cell is a special kind of battery that changes chemical energy directly into current electricity. Since 2005

Let There Be Light

In 1879 Thomas Edison invented a device that dramatically changed the world—the first practical electric lightbulb. In Edison's lightbulb, an electric current flowed through a thin coil of wire called a filament. The filament, a thread covered with carbon, would get so hot that it glowed white, giving off light. It lasted only forty-five minutes. Modern incandescent lightbulbs use a metal called tungsten as the filament. It not only glows brightly but can last for hundreds or thousands of hours.

Incandescent lightbulbs actually waste a lot of energy, because they produce a lot of heat in addition to the light. Fluorescent lights work differently. A stream of electrons flows through a tube filled with gas. The energy carried by the electrons makes the chemical coating the inside of the tube glow brightly (fluoresce). Fluorescence is a kind of energy change that produces mostly light and very little heat. And so, much less energy is wasted.

the U.S. government has been supporting research and development aimed at making fuel cells a practical energy source for cars and trucks. These fuel cells will use pure hydrogen as the fuel instead of gasoline.

In these batteries, hydrogen gas under pressure is split into hydrogen ions (H^+) and electrons. The electrons pass through the anode into the electrical circuits of the car. There they do useful work, such as turning a motor, and then return to the cathode of the fuel cell. Meanwhile, oxygen gas is forced into the cathode side of the fuel cell and split into oxygen

This sport-utility vehicle runs on a fuel cell. The fuel cell uses pure hydrogen to run the motor and, unlike other types of engines, does not pollute the air.

atoms. These atoms combine with hydrogen ions and electrons to form water. Unlike gasoline-burning engines, future cars powered by fuel cells will produce no pollution at all.

Electricity Inside Us

Did you know that you have electricity flowing through your body all the time? These electric currents aren't strong enough to hurt you. Your brain, for example, produces tiny electric currents so small that it would take about thirty million of them to light up a small flashlight bulb. Your body's electricity carries messages along nerves and muscles. When you read, your eyes send messages to your brain. When you smell flowers, your nose sends messages to your brain.

You don't feel the electric currents in your body. But scientists can use electrodes pasted to the skin to pick them up and machines to record them. In sleep labs, scientists can study people's brain waves. Doctors can use the body's electric currents to check on the workings of the heart, as well. They can even detect when someone is having a heart attack.

chapter three

Magnetic Energy

Thousands of years ago, people found that certain rocks have a mysterious force. These rocks contain an iron ore called magnetite, a dark, shiny, crystal-like material. They can attract and repel objects made of iron. If someone holds the rock over tiny pieces of iron, for example, the iron pieces will fly into the air and stick to the rock. This mysterious force is called magnetism. Materials that attract iron are called magnets.

About A.D. 1200, European scientists found that if they hung a piece of rock containing magnetite on a string, it would always point in the same direction—north. When they rubbed a thin, needle-shaped piece of iron on this strange rock, the magnetic force transferred to the needle. The needle itself then attracted other pieces of iron. They called this rock lodestone, which means "leading stone," and used it to make the world's first compass.

Early compasses consisted of a needle, magnetized by rubbing with a lodestone, and placed on a piece of wood floating in a tub of water. There it would turn to the north-south position. With a compass, sailors no longer had to steer their ships according to the Moon and stars. They could use compasses to find their way across oceans.

The Basics about Magnets

If you take a bar magnet and move it over a pile of tacks,

Lodestone (above) *is naturally magnetic. It was used in early compasses.*

the tacks will cling to the magnet. They will cluster mostly around the ends of the magnet, called poles, where the force is strongest. The end that points toward the north is called the north pole, and the end that points toward the south is called the south pole. The area around each pole, where the force acts on objects, is called a magnetic field.

When you move the north pole of one bar magnet near the north pole of another bar magnet, the magnets repel each other. The same thing happens if you put two south poles near each other. When the north pole of a magnet is near the south pole of another magnet, however, the two magnets attract each other and stick together tightly. Only force can move them apart. Scientists summarize this action: Like poles repel. Unlike poles attract. (Does that sound familiar? Remember the basic law of electricity: Like charges repel, and unlike charges attract.) The attraction (or repulsion) between two magnetic poles drops rather sharply as the distance between them increases.

What Makes a Magnet Magnetic?

Magnetism is caused by the movement of electrons inside atoms. In a material such as iron, the atoms gather together in clusters and line up to form groups called domains. Normally, these domains point in different directions and cancel one another out, so there is no magnetic field. But if the iron is magnetized by placing it next to another magnet, the domains line up in the same direction. They become parallel to one another and to the magnetic field. The individual fields of the domains then combine to form a single large one, and the metal becomes a magnet.

Once iron, nickel, and cobalt are magnetized, they remain magnetic. That is, they are permanent magnets. Some other substances can become magnetic when they are placed in a magnetic field, but they lose their magnetism when they are removed from the field.

Try picking up a paper clip with a magnet. Then get several other paper clips and bring them to the first paper clip. You will find that the paper clips will hang onto one another in a single line, dangling from the magnet. The entire line of paper clips has become magnetized. Is there a limit to the number of paper clips you can hold together magnetically? What happens if you use plastic- or rubber-coated paper clips instead of metal ones?

This magnet has magnetized the paper clips. Because they are magnetized, they pick up the next paper clip in line.

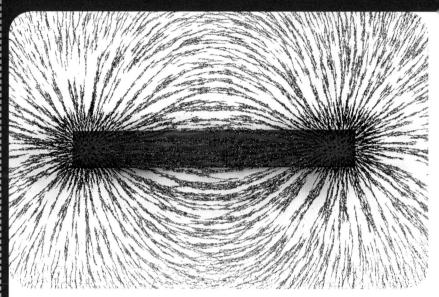

The iron filings sprinkled on this magnet trace the shape of its magnetic field.

Picturing the Lines of Magnetic Force

During the 1830s, British scientist Michael Faraday wondered how one magnetic pole could push or pull another across an empty space. He suggested that little threads, called "lines of magnetic force," join a magnet's north and south poles. When the opposite poles of two magnets are brought close to each other, the lines of magnetic force stretch from one pole across to the other, as if they were trying to pull the two poles together. When like poles of two magnets are placed near each other, the lines of one pole turn away from the lines of the other, pushing sideways and forcing the two poles apart.

A Close Link

For years, scientists suspected that electricity and magnetism were somehow related. In 1820 Danish physicist Hans Christian Oersted proved that there is indeed a close link between them. He called this connection electromagnetism. Oersted wanted to find out if an electric current would affect a magnetic compass. If it did, the compass needle would move.

In his classic experiment, Oersted placed a wire in a north-south direction. He laid a compass near the wire, with its needle parallel to the wire (which was also in a north-south direction). Then Oersted turned on a switch that started an electric current flowing through the wire. The needle moved to a different direction, at a right angle to the wire.

Faraday discovered a simple way to show the invisible lines of magnetic force. You can make a picture of a magnetic field by placing a piece of cardboard on top of a magnet. Sprinkle iron filings evenly over the cardboard and then tap it gently. (To make your own iron filings, rub a large iron nail with a file.) Although the magnetic field is continuous, interactions between the filings will cause them to make thin, curving lines of force on the cardboard.

When he reversed the direction of the current flow, the compass needle moved in the opposite direction, again at a right angle to the wire.

Oersted realized that the electric current created a magnetic field around the wire. The magnetic field then forced the compass needle to move. When he cut off the electric current, the needle went back to its normal north-south position.

French scientist André-Marie Ampère was fascinated with Oersted's experiment. He conducted some experiments of his own, to learn more about electromagnetism. In 1827 Ampère showed that an electric current flowing in a coil of wire increases the strength of the magnetic field. This led to the development of the electromagnet—a coil of wire wrapped around an iron bar that produced strong magnetic fields. Ampère's discovery became the basis for the development of the electric motor and the electric generator.

In 1831 Michael Faraday found not only that electricity could produce magnetism but also that magnetism could produce electricity. Faraday showed that when a magnet is moved through a closed coil of wire, it produces an electric current in the wire. This is known as electromagnetic induction. The magnetic field acted on the atoms in the wire, repelling electrons out of their orbits. The electrons then moved along the wire, creating an electric current. This discovery led to the invention of a device that could generate electricity—the alternating-current generator.

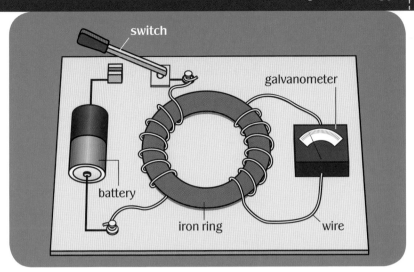

switch

galvanometer

battery

iron ring

wire

A galvanometer is an instrument for measuring electric current. When the switch is lowered, current flows through the left-hand coil, inducing a magnetic field around the iron ring. This changing magnetic field causes a momentary current to flow in the right-hand coil.

Before Faraday, scientists believed that electric currents flowed in only one direction—from the negatively charged end of a battery, for instance, to the positive end. This kind of flow of electricity is known as direct current (DC). Faraday proved that alternating current (AC) can also be generated. Alternating current changes direction. The electrons move in one direction and then alternate (change) and flow in the opposite direction.

Electromagnetism Is Everywhere

In modern times, we use Faraday's discovery to power most of the electrical devices that help shape our lives. Electric lights, refrigerators, microwave ovens, TV sets, and computers all run on alternating current.

Plugging the cord of a clock, a toaster, or a computer into an electric outlet creates an electric field around the wire and the device. This field exists even if the device is not turned on, and no current is flowing. (In that case, it is static electricity—a form of potential energy.)

The strength of an electric field depends on the voltage. The voltage is the difference in electric charge between one point in the circuit and another—for example, between a radio and the wall outlet that is holding its plug. In the United States, plug-in electrical devices run on electric current delivered at about 120 volts, the standard for alternating current. But many devices can run on the power stored in batteries, which lets them work while they are being carried around. Flashlights, radios, music players, electric shavers, toothbrushes, cameras, and other small portable devices typically run on batteries with a voltage of 9 volts or even less.

The current from a flashlight battery would not give you much of a shock, but sticking your fingers into an electrical wall outlet could really hurt. Imagine getting struck by a bolt of lightning, which delivers about 100 million volts! Many people die from lightning strikes every year. But amazingly, many others survive.

Flowing current produces not only electrical fields but also magnetic fields in the space around it. (If no current is flowing—such as in a radio that is plugged in but not turned on—there will be an electric field but no magnetic field.) The strength of both kinds

Electric Healing

"Code Blue!" The patient's heart has stopped beating. The emergency team dashes in with a crash cart and delivers a powerful shock to the patient's chest. This electrical jolt starts the heart beating again. The life-restoring electric current from a medical defibrillator has about 1,000 volts, much more powerful than ordinary room current. But low-power electromagnetism can have some medically useful effects, as well. It helps heal wounds and muscle strains. Electromagnets can also speed up the healing of broken bones.

of fields—electrical and magnetic—decreases sharply with distance. Sitting right up next to the TV screen, for example, puts you into its electromagnetic fields (EMF). But if you move back a few feet, you will be beyond the range of its electromagnetic effects.

Take a moment to picture your home. How many appliances and other electrical devices are there in each room? Next imagine the electromagnetic fields that all these devices are producing. You can't see, hear, or smell them, but they are there, surrounding each clock, radio, TV, and computer. Another source of EMF that you may not have thought of is the power line that delivers electricity to your home. Of course, it is farther away than your appliances, but it is also much more powerful.

Some people worry about the possible health effects of all these unseen but ever-present electromagnetic fields. They are especially concerned about devices that are very close to people while they are running—for example, electric blankets, blow dryers, electric shavers, toothbrushes, computers, and microwave ovens.

Some researchers have reported apparent links between EMFs and harmful health effects. They claimed that EMFs may change the body's cells and cause leukemia, brain tumors, breast and skin cancer, reproductive problems, and mood disorders such as depression. For example, Swedish scientists studied nearly half a million children in 1992. They reported that the children living close to power lines had a leukemia rate about four times as high as other children. Many other studies, however, have found no evidence of such health effects.

Is It Safe to Use Cell Phones?

Do you have a cell phone? If so, you're not alone. At least 60 percent of U.S. teenagers do, and the number of eight- to twelve-year-olds with their own cell phones is also growing rapidly. In fact, cell phones are not just for talking anymore. People use them to go on the Internet, text message their friends, play games, watch movies, and take pictures.

Some health experts are worried, though. A few studies have shown a possible link between heavy

We don't know all the answers yet, and scientists continue to research the effects of low-energy EMFs. Meanwhile, the World Health Organization (WHO) and national governments have set guidelines and safety standards for electrical devices. Manufacturers have added special shielding and other safety measures for TV sets, microwave ovens, and appliances. The guidelines are continually reviewed and changed as new information comes in. In the modern world, it is not easy to avoid EMFs—they are all around us.

cell phone use and brain cancer and other health problems. These handy little phones give off a form of electromagnetic radiation. The amounts of radiation are tiny, but they can affect living cells. Children and teenagers may be more sensitive than adults. And over time, the effects might build up. So far, most of the studies have not found any solid evidence of health risks. But cell phones have not been widely used long enough for long-term studies.

chapter four

Light Energy

Do you ever wonder why you see a rainbow of colors after a rain shower? Where do the colors come from? For thousands of years, rainbows have amazed and puzzled observers. English physicist Sir Isaac Newton explored this mysterious phenomenon.

In an experiment in 1666, Newton let a small beam of sunlight enter a darkened room. It passed through an angled piece of glass called a prism. As the light hit the prism, the light broke up into a rainbow of colors that blended into one another. Newton called this band of colors a spectrum. Newton found that when he passed each of these colors through other prisms, the colors did not change. But if he passed the whole band of colored lights through a prism that was turned around to the reverse position, the light that came out of the prism was white.

We cannot see sunlight. But as Newton found, white light actually contains all the colors in the rainbow. Newton examined each color in the white light. He realized that each part of the original beam is refracted (bent) by a different amount when it passes through the prism. This difference in the bending makes the colors stand out, allowing them to be visible to the human eye.

When sunlight shines through raindrops, it splits into the different colors of the spectrum. This split creates a rainbow.

A rainbow is actually a spectrum formed when sunlight shines through raindrops, which act as prisms. The Sun's rays hit the raindrops and, depending on the angle, the colors of the spectrum are produced—red, orange, yellow, green, blue (sometimes indigo is included), and violet. The colored light is then reflected, or mirrored back, to our eyes.

Why Is the Sky Blue?

Although sunlight contains all the colors, we see only blue when we look up at the sky on a clear, sunny day. That's because of the way Earth's atmosphere reflects light. The air molecules absorb the light energy of nearly all the colors we can see. But blue light is reflected and scattered across the sky.

Where Does Light Come From?

Light is a form of energy, often called radiant energy. All light is radiated (given off) by the electrons circling the nucleus of their atom. Electrons revolve around the nucleus in certain patterns called orbitals. Electrons close to the nucleus have less energy than those in orbitals farther out.

Electrons that are in the lowest energy level do not give off any light. If an atom is heated, however, the electrons in lower energy levels gain energy and move faster. They may then jump to a higher energy level. Then the atom is said to be excited. The excited electron may then lose energy and fall back to a lower level. The gaining and losing of energy causes the atoms to radiate light in small packets called photons. The spectrum of lights with different colors is made up of photons with different amounts of energy.

How Does Light Travel?

As sunlight showers over Earth, it moves in waves like the waves of the ocean. But light energy can travel not only through a substance like the ocean but also through air or even a vacuum such as space.

Light waves are called electromagnetic waves because they are made up of electrical and magnetic fields that travel together. The electrical field moves up and down while the magnetic field moves back and forth.

Waves or Particles?

In the seventeenth century, scientists argued about exactly what light is. Is it made up of tiny particles, or does it travel in waves? Isaac Newton believed that light is the result of tiny particles given off by light sources, such as the Sun. Dutch physicist Christiaan Huygens, on the other hand, suggested that light consists of waves. By 1900 scientists had learned that light can act like either particles or waves. They were both right.

The colored lights of a rainbow represent only one type of electromagnetic radiation. Visible light belongs to a much larger spectrum of energy called the electromagnetic spectrum. Visible light is just the small part of the spectrum that can be seen by the human eye. We cannot see the rest of the spectrum.

Every electromagnetic wave has a specific length, known as the wavelength—the distance between the top of one wave and the top of the next. The wave also has a specific height, known as the amplitude. The amplitude is related to the strength of the electric and magnetic fields and to the number of photons the light contains.

The number of waves that pass a given point in a certain amount of time is known as the frequency. All electromagnetic waves move at the same speed—about 186,000 miles (300,000 kilometers) per second. So the number of short waves that pass by a given point is greater than the number of long waves that pass in the same amount of time.

At one end of the electromagnetic spectrum, the wavelengths are long and spread out. At the other end of the spectrum, the waves are smaller and closer together. The smaller the wavelength, the greater the energy. Radio waves have the longest wavelength in the spectrum and give off the least amount of energy. The other radiations, in order along the spectrum, are microwaves, infrared radiation, visible light, ultraviolet radiation, X-rays and, finally, gamma rays. Gamma rays have the shortest wavelengths and contain the greatest amount of energy.

Radio waves are all around us. Although we cannot see or hear them, they carry information for radio and television broadcasts; telephones; and radio communication in taxicabs, planes, and emergency vehicles. In a radio broadcast, sounds spoken or played into a microphone are changed first into

Waves can be measured by their wavelength or by their frequency. The wavelength of light determines what color the light appears—or doesn't appear.

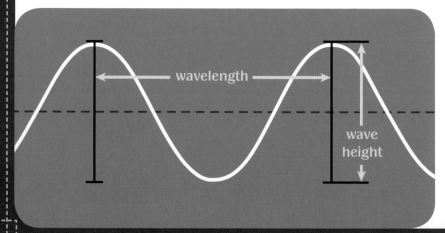

Energy

electrical signals and
then into radio waves
that are broadcast from
huge transmitters. The
radio that you use to
listen to the news or
music is an electrical
device that changes
radio waves into sounds.

Microwaves are used
to cook food. These
long waves make the
water molecules in food
move around. As the
molecules bump against
one another, they
produce friction and a
lot of heat. This heat
then cooks the food.

Microwave ovens use microwaves to heat food quickly.

Infrared radiation is often called heat radiation because it is
released by most hot objects. Special glasses called night vision
goggles change some wavelengths and allow people to see
objects in the dark, from the heat radiation they give off.

Visible light is the only portion of the electromagnetic
spectrum that we can see. We can distinguish the whole
rainbow of colors and hundreds of shades in between.

Ultraviolet radiation is often called black light. We cannot
see it, but when it falls on certain chemicals it produces changes
in their electron energy levels. These chemicals then give off
radiations of their own, in the visible range. Some animals

are able to see ultraviolet radiation. Bumblebees, for instance, can see colors in flowers that we cannot see.

X-rays are commonly used in doctors' offices to diagnose broken bones. They are invisible waves that pass right through skin, muscles, and organs but are reflected off bones and teeth. The bones are so dense that they show up on the X-ray film. Depending on the wavelength, time of exposure, and the way they are processed, X-ray images can

Beam Me Up, Scotty!

Will we ever have instant transporters, like those on the TV and movie series *Star Trek*? In 1997 Austrian researchers reported what may be the first step in developing this science-fiction-like technology. They destroyed some photons and transferred the information about their key characteristics to other photons 3 feet (1 meter) away. These other photons became perfect copies of the photons that had disappeared. The researchers think that in the early twenty-first century, they can learn to apply this "quantum teleportation" to atoms and even molecules. As for people and other living organisms— it's theoretically possible, but it's not going to happen very soon.

also show organs such as the heart and lungs.

Gamma radiation is produced in changes that occur inside the nuclei (the plural of nucleus) of atoms. In some elements, such as uranium and thorium, these changes occur naturally. They are radioactive and

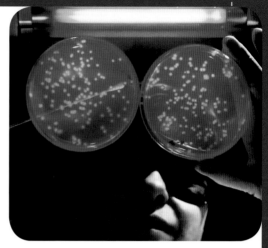

This scientist is using a black light to see the microorganisms used in her experiment.

continually give off gamma rays and other forms of radiation. These radiations are also released in nuclear explosions. Gamma rays are similar to X-rays but even shorter in wavelength and higher in energy. They can damage cells and tissues. In large doses, they can be very harmful to people exposed to them.

In the electromagnetic spectrum, radio waves have the longest wavelength and gamma rays have the shortest. Visible light falls in the middle.

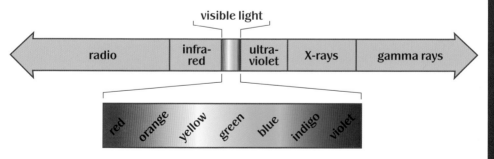

visible light

radio | infra-red | ultra-violet | X-rays | gamma rays

red orange yellow green blue indigo violet

· increasing energy and frequency   · decreasing wavelength

The World's Most Important Light Source

Our most important source of light energy is the Sun. Energy from the Sun is called solar energy. Nearly all living things depend on solar energy to live—directly or indirectly.

The Sun provides food for many living things. Plants, for example, use sunlight for photosynthesis. During this process, the plants absorb the Sun's light energy and use it to produce chemical reactions. Using the energy of sunlight, carbon dioxide and water are turned into food materials such as sugars, starches, and other carbohydrates. Meanwhile, some energy is stored in a chemical compound called adenosine triphosphate (ATP). ATP provides a ready source of energy for a variety of chemical reactions. Any excess energy is stored in more complex chemicals, starches, and fats.

Animals that eat plants are consuming energy that came originally from sunlight. They break down plant chemicals to use as building materials for their own bodies. They also burn sugars

Did You Know?

The green color of plants comes from a green chemical called chlorophyll. It acts as a sort of antenna, gathering energy to be used in photosynthesis. Actually, green light is practically the only kind of visible light that chlorophyll does *not* absorb. It looks green because it reflects green light back to our eyes.

and fats for energy to power their movements and chemical reactions. Like plants, animals use ATP to store small amounts of energy for short periods of time.

Plants release energy through a process called respiration. Respiration is actually the opposite of photosynthesis. While photosynthesis occurs only during the daytime when there is sunlight, respiration occurs throughout the day and night. During respiration, glucose, a type of sugar stored in the plant,

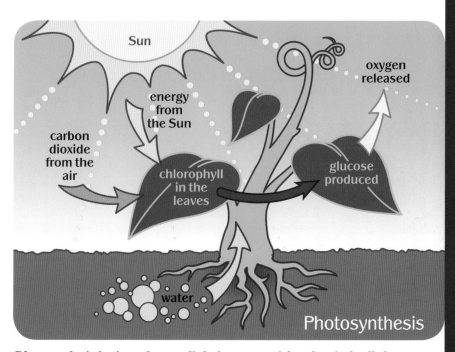

Photosynthesis

Photosynthesis begins when sunlight interacts with a chemical called chlorophyll in the plant's leaves to produce light energy that is stored as chemical energy. Carbon dioxide and water also enter the leaf and combine with the energy stored to produce glucose (sugar), which is either stored, used right away for energy, or used to make other food substances.

combines with oxygen to release energy. This is a chemical reaction, much like the release of energy from coal or fuel oil when it burns in the presence of oxygen. In respiration, glucose is burned in the presence of oxygen, producing carbon dioxide and

Miniature Powerhouses

Energy for our bodies' activities is produced in each cell inside tiny football-shaped structures, called mitochondria. Respiration takes place here, burning sugars and producing energy-rich ATP. The mitochondria are actually somewhat similar to the structures in plant cells called chloroplasts. Chloroplasts store energy from sunlight in sugars and other complex chemicals.

Both the mitochondria and the chloroplasts have their own sets of genetic information. This genetic information is inherited separately from the genes that carry the plans for all the other traits of the organism. In fact, many scientists believe that mitochondria and chloroplasts were once independent bacteria-like creatures. They are thought to have been captured by large cells and then worked for those cells in return for a sheltered place to live.

water as by-products. The chemical energy released from the sugar is temporarily stored in ATP.

Sunlight—Good and Bad

While plants need the Sun to make their own food, animals depend indirectly on the Sun's energy. Plant-eating animals use the plant energy to live. Animals that eat other animals use the energy that was originally produced by the plants. Humans are also learning to capture and store sunlight energy and convert it to chemical, heat, and electrical energy. This solar energy can then be used to heat our buildings and power our machines.

Solar energy gives us many benefits. But too much exposure to sunlight can be harmful. The ultraviolet radiation in sunlight can cause sunburn in people who stay out in the sun too long. Overexposure to sunlight may cause faster aging of the skin, eye disorders, and skin cancer, as well.

Fortunately, most of the ultraviolet radiation given off by the Sun is absorbed by the ozone layer in Earth's atmosphere. But pollution produced by human activities has damaged the ozone layer. This protective layer has been rapidly thinning or disappearing completely in some parts. Efforts are being made to reduce pollution and therefore slow down or reverse the loss of our protective ozone shield.

chapter five

Heat Energy

Where would we be if early humans had not learned how to make fire? Chances are, we would all be living near the equator, where the Sun's radiant energy keeps the planet's surface warm all year-round. After fire was discovered, people began moving to colder climates. From the distant past to modern day, heat has become a very important source of energy. We use heat energy to warm our homes, cook our meals, and make appliances and machinery work.

In fact, all other kinds of energy are at some point converted to heat energy. Sunlight, converted to heat, warms the lands and oceans. A car's engine uses electrical energy, which is turned into mechanical energy, which is converted to heat energy. A lightbulb is powered by electrical energy, which heats up the metal wire inside until it glows with light. A toaster uses electrical energy to produce heat, which converts bread to toast. Ovens and clothes dryers may be powered either by electricity or by burning gas, a chemical reaction that gives off heat.

What Makes Things Hot?

Heat energy is simply the movement of molecules in matter. All matter contains atoms or molecules that are always moving with kinetic energy. These moving particles give every object internal energy. If the atoms or molecules are moving very fast, then the object has a high level of internal energy. If the atoms or molecules are moving very slowly, then the object has a low level of internal energy. The higher the internal energy, the hotter the object.

People often describe things as hot or cold. What they are really describing is the temperature of an object, measured

Experiment: What's the Temperature?

Can you always tell when something is hot or cold? When we walk outside on a hot summer day, our bodies can feel that it is very warm. On cold winter days, our bodies can tell that it is very cold outside. But we are not always good thermometers for determining what is really hot and cold.

This can be shown in an experiment. Fill three bowls with water at three different temperatures: one hot, one cold, and one warm. Put one hand in the hot water and the other in cold water for a few seconds. Then put both hands in the warm water. Each hand will tell you something different. The hand that was in hot water will feel very cold in the warm water, but the one that was in cold water will feel very hot.

by a thermometer. Temperature is measured mainly in two units: degrees Fahrenheit (°F) and degrees Celsius (°C). The Fahrenheit scale is commonly used in the United States for everyday household purposes, such as the temperature of an oven, a room, or the outdoors. In this temperature scale, water freezes at 32°F and boils at 212°F. The Celsius scale, part of the metric system, is used for scientific measurements. It was set up so that the freezing point of water is 0°C, and its boiling point is 100°C. Nearly all countries use the Celsius scale to calculate temperature.

The Fahrenheit and Celsius scales are good for most purposes, but in certain scientific calculations it is better to use an absolute temperature scale. In this scale, 0° corresponds to absolute zero—a point so cold that all motion, even that inside atoms, has stopped. The absolute scale corresponding to Celsius temperatures is called the Kelvin scale, and its unit is °K. Zero degrees Kelvin is the same as −273.16°C.

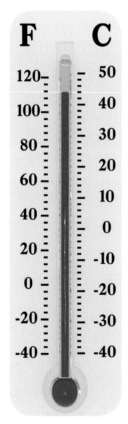

This thermometer shows both the Fahrenheit and Celsius scales.

The Changing States of Water

Increasing temperature causes water to change its state, from solid to liquid to gas. Ice is solid water. Its atoms are packed together, moving so slightly that the ice keeps its shape. When heated, the atoms in the ice start to move around more and the bonds between molecules loosen. The ice starts melting.

The atoms or molecules in a liquid move around somewhat independently of one another, but they are not totally free. As the particles move over one another, the liquid flows, molding itself to the shape of its container.

When water is heated, say, in a pot on the stove, the water molecules gain energy and move more and more rapidly. At the boiling point, the water molecules have so much energy that they free themselves from one another. The particles then

Left: *The atoms in these ice cubes are more tightly packed than the atoms in the water.* **Right:** *The atoms in steam, a gaseous form of water, are less tightly packed than the atoms in water.*

start flying through the air. The kinetic energy in the boiling water causes the water to turn to steam. Like other gases, steam can expand as it is heated. If the pot has a lid on it, the steam may push against the lid, making it rattle.

Why Do We Shiver and Sweat?

Your body responds to changes in temperature in different ways. If you walk outside without a jacket on a cold winter day, your body may start to shiver (shake). What happens is that the blood vessels in your muscles start to shrink and then relax. This makes the muscles contract (shrink by squeezing together), producing heat as a by-product. By shivering, your body is actually trying to warm up.

When your body is overheated on a hot summer day, the blood vessels in your muscles start to expand. Your body then releases heat energy by sweating. The liquid water in sweat absorbs a lot of heat as it evaporates (turns into water vapor) and carries this heat away from the body. When the air is very humid, however, it already contains about as much water vapor as it can hold. Sweat can't evaporate, so sweating does not cool you as well.

If steam touches something cold, its heat energy goes into the cold object, and the steam changes back into liquid water. This change is called condensation.

A liquid can turn into a gas even without boiling. A puddle on the sidewalk gradually disappears when the Sun comes out. The warm rays of sunlight turn liquid water into a gas (water vapor). Rubbing alcohol dabbed on your hand disappears even more quickly, as the liquid changes into a vapor. The change from the liquid to the gas state is called evaporation. Like melting from a solid to a liquid, this change uses energy.

The Transfer of Heat Energy

Heat energy can flow in only one direction—from a hot object to a cold object. Heat energy is transferred from one object to another in three ways: conduction, convection, and radiation.

Conduction is the direct transfer of heat through a substance. For example, when the end of a copper rod is placed into a fire, it quickly becomes hot. Remember that heat energy is the movement of atoms or molecules. The atoms in the hot end start to vibrate faster and then hit surrounding atoms. These atoms move even faster and hit other atoms. The heat energy travels from atom to atom until it reaches the other end of the rod, even though not one copper atom has moved very far.

Convection is the transfer of heat by the movement of a heated substance. For example, in the winter you may use a space heater to warm up a room. It works much more quickly than if it were just transferring heat from hot molecules to others in contact with them. As air molecules around the heater are warmed, they move faster and spread out more. The air then becomes less dense (lighter) than the air around it and rises. Cooler air falls to take its place, and swirling currents of moving air soon spread out through the whole room. These convection currents continually bring more air molecules closer to the heater, where they are warmed in turn.

Radiation is the movement of heat energy through empty space. Waves of radiant energy move outward from a hot object. When radiant energy hits an object, it speeds up the atoms or molecules in that object. The Sun's energy is an example of radiant energy. Rays of sunlight warm Earth's surface. From the places where the Sun's rays strike, heat is further spread out by conduction in the ground and convection currents in the atmosphere.

A space heater (left) *uses convection to warm up a room. Sunlight* (right) *warms Earth's surface by radiation.*

This construction worker is placing insulation in the ceiling of a house. The insulation will reduce the flow of heat energy, making the house easier to keep warm in the winter and cool in the summer.

Heat Control

Your house can stay warm and comfortable in the winter if it is well insulated. Just as electrical insulators can block the flow of electricity, materials that do not conduct heat can control the flow of heat energy. For example, layers of fiberglass or other fluffy material inside the walls of houses hold heat inside in the winter and keep it outside in the summer. Both heaters and air conditioners work much more efficiently in a well-insulated house.

Laws of Thermodynamics

In the eighteenth and especially the nineteenth centuries, the Industrial Revolution changed the lives of people on our planet. Machines were invented to do heavy jobs that could only be done before by muscle power. Most of these machines were powered by the energy released by burning fuel. Scientists trying to improve these machines learned a great deal about how heat is converted to other

This illustration of 1870s Great Britain shows the large number of factories that were built during the Industrial Revolution. These factories burned fuels to do work that would previously have required many workers.

types of energy (and the reverse) and how heat can be made to do work. These studies formed a new branch of physics, called thermodynamics. Scientists came up with three laws of thermodynamics. They describe the relationships between heat and other forms of energy.

The first law of thermodynamics states that energy in a system, as simple as a ball or as complex as a machine, cannot be created nor destroyed. Energy is either changed from one form into another or transferred from one system to another. For example, your body is like a machine. You need fuel, in the form of food, to make your mind and body run. When you take a bite out of a hamburger and chew it up into little pieces, you use mechanical energy to make your jaws move.

Chewing is part of the process that provides your body with fuel. It also takes mechanical energy.

Enzymes (reactive chemicals) in your saliva start up chemical reactions, breaking the bits of hamburger into food chemicals. Digestion continues in the stomach and intestines. Some of the energy from the food is stored chemically, in ATP. Some is released in the form of heat. Food energy can also be turned into mechanical energy to move muscles for walking or lifting things. Therefore, we go through various energy conversions every time we eat a meal.

The second law of thermodynamics states that as energy is converted from one form to another, only a small amount of heat energy can do useful work. Most of the energy is released into the surroundings as heat. This lost energy is known as entropy. For example, in a car's engine, the chemical energy of gasoline is converted to heat energy. Part of this heat

The heat energy being released from this jet engine blurs the landscape. Only a small amount of the energy produced in an engine is useful. The rest is released as heat. This lost energy is called entropy.

Energy

energy causes the gas inside the engine to expand and push on the pistons, which convert the heat energy to mechanical energy. But much of the energy released from gasoline just heats up the engine. (In other words, it is entropy. In fact, this lost heat energy makes the car even less efficient. As the entropy builds up, a cooling system has to work—using up energy—to prevent damage to the engine.)

Meanwhile, the mechanical energy of the pistons is transferred to the tires, which push against the road surface and move the car. But the entropy increases here too. Friction between the tires and the road changes some of this mechanical energy to heat, which does no useful work and wears down the tire treads. The entropy in our world is constantly increasing because of energy-wasting processes like these.

The third law of thermodynamics concerns absolute zero. At this temperature, theoretically, all substances would have zero energy and zero entropy as well. However, the third law states that no matter how closely absolute zero is approached, it can never be reached.

chapter six

Sound Energy

We live in a world of sound. Sound lets us communicate with one another through speech. We enjoy the sounds that come from music and singing birds. We depend on the sounds that come from radio and television, providing us with entertainment and information. Sounds such as car horns and fire alarms warn us of danger. Other sounds may seem just plain annoying— like the noise of garbage cans banging together or the buzz of your alarm clock. Whether we like or dislike the sounds in our lives, they are everywhere.

What Is Sound?

When a guitar string is plucked, it moves back and forth. This movement is called a vibration. When the string vibrates, it presses on molecules in the surrounding air. Normally these gas molecules are spread out, but the vibration pushes them closer together (compresses them). These molecules bump into one another and then hit neighboring molecules. The vibration is transmitted outward from the

When you listen to someone play a guitar, you hear the vibration that started when the player plucked or strummed the strings.

string, creating waves in the air molecules. When some of the vibrating air molecules hit your eardrum, you can hear a sound.

All sounds make vibrations. If you touch your throat while you are talking, you can feel your vocal cords making vibrations. Without vibrations, sound cannot exist.

How Does Sound Travel?

Like light energy, sound energy travels in waves. Sound waves are called compression waves. The molecules in the air are compressed when they vibrate. A vibrating object sends out sound waves in all directions.

Sound must travel through a medium, which may be a gas (such as air), a liquid, or a solid. Although we usually hear sounds traveling through the air, sound actually travels faster through a liquid or a solid than through a gas. That is because gas molecules do not vibrate as fast as those in a liquid or a solid. In fact, the speed of sound is about four times faster through water than through air and about fifteen times faster through steel. Have you ever seen a movie about the Old West in which a scout puts his ear to the ground to hear the distant hoofbeats of horses? He does this because sound travels faster through the solid ground than it does through the air.

Since sound energy needs a medium to travel and light energy does not, light travels much faster than sound. During a thunderstorm, you can tell just about

Silence in Space

Have you ever watched the TV show *Star Trek*? In episodes when the U.S.S. *Enterprise* battles with an alien ship, viewers could hear the sound of blasts coming from the phasers firing between the two ships. But that is not scientifically accurate. Sound can travel only if molecules are there, and no molecules exist in space. So it is impossible for phasers to give off sound in space. Similarly, real-life astronauts cannot talk to one another directly when they are on the Moon. Instead, they must communicate by radio, because radio waves, like light waves, can travel through the vacuum of space.

Energy

Although lightning and thunder start out at the same place, the lightning reaches you first because light travels much faster than sound.

how far away the lightning is by counting the seconds between the lightning flash and the rumbling thunder. Each five seconds you count means about 1 mile (1.6 km) of distance. Even though both the lightning and the thunder started out at the same time, the light reaches you much sooner. Light can travel at a speed of about 186,000 miles (300,000 km) per second, while sound travels at a speed of only 1,100 feet (335 m) per second.

The speed of sound may also depend on the temperature of the medium. Sound travels faster in warm air than in cold air because the air molecules move faster. For instance, sound travels 1,085 feet (331 m) per second through air at 32°F (0°C) and 1,268 feet (386 m) per second through air at 212°F (100°C).

The Nature of Sound

The nature of a sound is determined by its wavelength. A wavelength is the distance between one compression (wave peak) to the next one. The number of waves produced by a vibrating object each second is called the frequency of the sound waves. The faster an object vibrates, the greater the frequency. As the frequency increases, the wavelength decreases.

Scientists use the unit hertz (abbreviated Hz) to measure frequency. It is equal to one cycle per second. Most people can hear sounds from about 20 to 20,000 Hz. A person's voice can produce frequencies from 85 to 1,100 Hz. Animals such as bats, dogs, and dolphins can hear sounds with frequencies far above 20,000 Hz. These high frequencies are called ultrasounds because they are beyond human hearing.

The frequency of a sound determines its pitch—how high or low a sound seems to a listener. High-pitched sounds have higher frequencies than low-pitched sounds. When you turn an electric fan on low, its blades move rather slowly, and you hear a low-pitched hum. If you turn the fan up to a higher setting, the blades turn more rapidly, causing the air molecules around them to vibrate faster. This produces a higher-frequency sound wave, and you hear a higher-pitched hum. (What do the high-pitched whine of a mosquito and the lower-pitched buzz of a bee tell you about how fast their wings flap?)

"Silent" Sounds

Bats can hear ultrasound frequencies and use them to their advantage. For example, insect-eating bats can find prey in the dark without bumping into anything. A bat produces ultrasonic squeaks that reflect off obstacles and come back to the bat's ears. The reflection is called an echo. By interpreting the reflected sounds, the bat can detect objects in its path, including prey.

The process that bats use to find their prey is called echolocation. The sonar used by whales, dolphins, and ships to locate things underwater works on a similar principle. So does the radar used by aircraft, except that the signals and reflections are bouncing radio waves instead of sound waves.

Bats hear so well that they can use their ears instead of their eyes to hunt their prey. The ultrasonic squeaks they produce bounce off other objects allowing bats to sense what is in front of them.

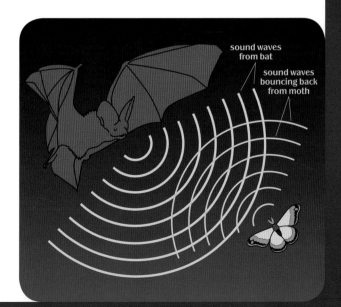

sound waves
from bat

sound waves
bouncing back
from moth

How Do We Hear?

How do sound waves translate into specific sounds that we can understand? When your mother calls you from the next room to come to dinner, her vocal cords vibrate and make sound waves that travel through the air. Some of the vibrating air molecules bump against your eardrum. The vibrations are then transmitted into the inner ear, where they stimulate nerve cells. Nerve cells change the sound energy to electrical energy, which is sent to a special hearing center in the brain. When the brain receives the signals, it translates them into sound.

Why does your own voice, played back on a tape recorder, usually sound different? When you speak, you hear your voice both through sound waves in the air and through vibrations transmitted by the bones of your skull. When you play a tape of your recorded voice, you hear only the waves that travel through the air.

When sound waves vibrate, each molecule moves back and forth from its original position. The distance that a vibrating object moves from its position at rest is called the amplitude of the sound wave. The amplitude of a sound wave determines the intensity of the sound—that is, the amount of energy that flows through the sound waves. The greater the amplitude of the vibration, the more intense the sound. The more intense a sound becomes, the louder it seems.

Making Use of Sound Energy

For centuries, doctors have listened to the sounds from patients' hearts and lungs to help diagnose illnesses. Modern high-tech instruments have expanded the doctor's range. Doctors use pictures made from reflected ultrasounds to diagnose brain tumors, gallstones, and other disorders. They also use ultrasounds to check on the development of fetuses.

A doctor uses an ultrasound to check the health of a fetus (unborn baby).

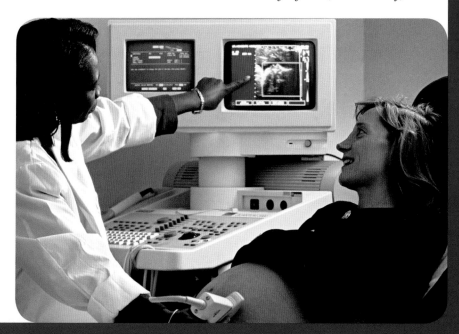

Scientists and engineers have created devices that can record and reproduce sound. A tape recorder records sounds on a cassette tape by changing sound energy into electrical energy. The tape is made of a plastic coated with iron powder. The microphone in the tape recorder changes the sound into electrical signals, which magnetize the iron powder on the tape. When the tape is played, the recorded magnetic signals are changed back into electric signals, which can be turned into sound with the help of speakers.

Sound Technology

To record sounds on a CD (compact disc), the sound waves are converted into a series of numbers by taking samples of the wave 44,100 times each second. These numbers are pressed into the plastic disc as microscopic bumps along a spiral track. The track starts at the middle of the disc and spirals outward to the outer edge. A source of laser light, moved by a motor, tracks the pattern of bumps along the spiral track. (If the spiral track on a typical CD were stretched out straight, it would be nearly 3.5 miles [5 km] long but less than 0.00002 inch [0.5 micrometer] wide.) Light energy is converted to electrical energy and then to sound energy to play the CD.

When you listen to music on the radio, the radio station also changes sound into electrical waves. The electrical waves send radio signals into the air. The antenna on your radio picks up the radio waves, which are then changed back into sounds that you can hear.

Similar energy changes occur to produce the sounds in television broadcasts. Meanwhile, the video cameras convert the light energy reflected from the actors and background into electrical waves. These waves may be changed into radio waves that are bounced off a satellite circling Earth out in space. Or the electrical signals may be transmitted over cables to the individual TV sets. Finally, they are changed back into light waves to produce the images on the screen.

chapter seven

Nuclear Energy

When people hear the term *nuclear energy*, they usually think about one of the world's most horrifying events. In August 1945, to end World War II (1939–1945), the United States dropped an atomic bomb on the Japanese city of Hiroshima. The blast was so powerful that it destroyed about 5 square miles (12 sq. km) of Hiroshima, killed thousands of people, and injured thousands of others. Thousands more were killed when the United States dropped another atomic bomb on the city of Nagasaki after the Japanese government did not surrender after the first one.

In an atomic bomb, nuclear energy is released in an explosion, and the results are devastating. Although nuclear energy is the most powerful kind of energy, it is not always harmful. Scientists have found ways to release nuclear energy more slowly, under strict control. With these safeguards, it is an important power source that provides us with electricity.

The atomic bomb that was dropped on Nagasaki, Japan, created this dense column of smoke, known as a mushroom cloud. The devastation caused by the bomb was widespread.

What Is Nuclear Energy?

While chemical energy involves reactions that take place outside the nucleus of an atom, nuclear energy involves reactions that take place inside the nucleus. As you recall, nuclei contain two kinds of particles: protons, which have a positive charge, and neutrons, which are electrically neutral. Almost all the weight of an atom is in the protons and neutrons. The electrons whizzing through the space around the nuclei are far smaller.

The number of protons in an atom's nucleus (which is the same as the number of electrons) is called the atomic number of the element. Every chemical element has its own atomic number. The total number of protons and neutrons in an atom's nucleus is called the mass number of the element. For example, the lightest element, hydrogen, has only one proton and no neutrons. Therefore, hydrogen's atomic number and mass number are both 1. Oxygen has eight protons and eight neutrons, so its atomic number is 8 and its mass number is 16.

The atoms of an element may have different weights but share the same chemical properties. Most hydrogen nuclei, for instance, contain one proton and no neutrons. But other varieties include deuterium, with one proton and one neutron, and tritium, with one proton and two neutrons. The various forms of an element are called isotopes. Isotopes of an element all have the same atomic number (one in the case of hydrogen) but different atomic masses.

Most elements have at least one isotope in addition to their common form. Uranium, one of the heaviest elements, has fourteen isotopes. Each uranium isotope has an atomic number of 92 (that is, it has 92 protons). The heaviest uranium isotope has 146 neutrons. This means that the combination of protons and neutrons makes a mass number of 238. This isotope is called

This is uranium ore. Uranium is one of the heaviest elements, and it has an unstable nucleus.

uranium 238, or U-238. It is somewhat unstable and can undergo nuclear reactions. It is referred to as a radioisotope because it gives off radiations when it breaks down.

What Happens in a Nuclear Reaction?

In a nuclear reaction, the nuclei of atoms are broken apart or joined together. This can happen naturally, or the reaction may be set off by introducing a lot of energy from an outside source. During the nuclear reaction, some of the mass of the reacting atoms is changed to energy. Scientist Albert Einstein proved that a tiny amount of mass can be converted to a huge amount of energy. That is why nuclear reactions can be used in bombs to destroy things or, in more controlled reactions, to produce electric power.

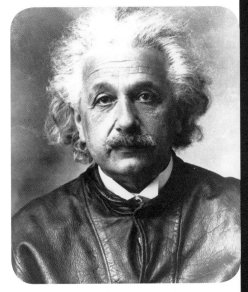

All the elements except for the simplest one, hydrogen, have more than one proton in the nucleus. Normally, protons would repel one another because they all have the same electrical charge. However, the protons and neutrons in an atomic nucleus are all held together by a nuclear force, which is even stronger than the electrical force.

Albert Einstein (1879–1955) changed the way scientists look at energy.

Generally, small nuclei are more stable than larger ones because the nuclear force works best over small distances. If the nuclear force is weak, then the nucleus is unstable—it will naturally decay, or break apart, into smaller groups of particles.

An atom whose nucleus is unstable is radioactive. When the nucleus decays, the atom is changed to one of a different isotope or even a different element. As the nuclei break apart, they release radiation. Three types of radiation may be released in a nuclear reaction: alpha particles (consisting of two protons and two neutrons), beta particles (electrons), and gamma rays.

Nuclear Medicine

In a special field of medicine called nuclear medicine, doctors use radioisotopes to study, diagnose, and treat patients. For instance, doctors can detect an abnormal brain growth called a tumor. A small amount of radioisotope is injected into the body. Instruments called scanners can detect the radiation. They make an image of body tissues that have taken up the largest amounts of the radioisotope.

Radioisotopes can also be used to treat cancers. Large amounts of radiation can kill living tissues, especially dividing cells. Cancer cells divide more

This man is undergoing a radiation treatment. The machine bombards his body with radioisotopes, which are meant to kill his cancer.

often than healthy ones, so radiation kills more cancerous cells than normal ones.

People who have been exposed to high amounts of certain types of radiation may get radiation sickness. The radiation may come from nuclear explosions, such as atom and hydrogen bombs, medical and industrial uses of radioisotopes, or X-ray machines. The radiation may cause serious damage to the body's cells, resulting in lasting injury or even death. Doctors often treat radiation sickness with blood transfusions and antibiotics to fight infection.

Scientists measure the rate of radioactive decay in a unit of time called a half-life. That is the amount of time it takes for half of the atoms of a particular radioisotope to decay into another element or isotope. The heavier the atom, the longer it takes to decay. Tritium, the heaviest form of hydrogen, is a radioactive isotope that has a half-life of about twelve years. Uranium 238 is a much heavier radioisotope that takes a much longer time to decay—its half-life is about 5 billion years!

Nuclear Fission

Nuclear fission is a more powerful kind of nuclear reaction than radioactive decay—more energy is released. Heavy nuclei are split into two or more large parts, called fission fragments. Most of the energy is released as heat, the rest as radiation.

Atomic bombs use nuclear fission reactions of two isotopes of uranium, U-238 and U-235. Uranium occurs naturally in rocks. However, there is no danger that a chunk of uranium ore will explode. U-238 and U-235 make up only a small portion of the uranium in rocks.

Scientists can split uranium nuclei by bombarding them with neutrons. Uranium 238 and uranium 235 release neutrons when they undergo nuclear fission. These extra neutrons hit other uranium nuclei and cause them to split. This process is repeated over and over, and it becomes an ongoing chain reaction, in which one reaction causes another one to occur. For a chain reaction to continue, the uranium must have a critical mass. This is the smallest amount of uranium that will keep a chain reaction going.

Nuclear Fusion

In nuclear fission, very heavy nuclei break into two lighter parts. In nuclear fusion, on the other hand, two light nuclei fuse (join together) to form a heavier nucleus. Fusion reactions are far more powerful because much more mass is changed to energy than in fission reactions. Unlike fission, fusion does not produce radioactive isotopes, so it is safer.

But fusion is also more difficult to produce. Normally, atomic nuclei are surrounded by electrons. So how can nuclei get past the electrons of other nuclei to join together? The electrons must be stripped away from the nuclei for the fusion process to occur. To do this, fusion reactions require extremely high temperatures—about 32 million °F (18 million °C) and higher. These high temperatures are needed to give the nuclei enough energy to join together when they collide. This reaction is called a thermonuclear fusion reaction.

Thermonuclear fusion reactions are produced artificially in hydrogen bombs. An atomic fission bomb is used as a trigger to make enough heat for fusion reactions to occur.

How Safe Is Nuclear Energy?

The atom and hydrogen bombs are examples of nuclear energy released in reactions that get out of control. However, nuclear

How Hot Is the Sun?

The temperature on the Sun's surface is about 10,000°F (5,500°C) and more than 25 million °F (13.9 million °C) in the center. Compare those huge numbers to the hottest temperature ever recorded on Earth: 136°F (58°C) in Al' Aziziyah, Libya, in September 1922. The great amount of energy needed to produce the high temperatures of the Sun and other stars comes from thermonuclear reactions that take place inside them. Fusion reactions occur at these high temperatures. Inside the Sun, hydrogen burns. Deuterium fuses with tritium, forming a helium nucleus and releasing large amounts of energy.

energy can be produced in controlled reactions in nuclear reactors, so it can be used for practical purposes. Nuclear power plants use nuclear fission reactions, with U-235 and U-238 for fuel.

In addition to uranium rods, the reactor contains neutron-absorbing rods called control rods. Inserted among or removed from the uranium rods, they control the reaction by absorbing neutrons and keeping a chain reaction from starting. The slower the nuclear reaction, the easier it is to direct the energy into useful work.

In April 1986, an awful accident occurred at the Chernobyl nuclear power plant in Ukraine in Eastern Europe. A reactor, running with its safety features turned off, melted down, spewing dangerous radioactive materials over not only the local area but surrounding countries as well. In addition to those injured and killed in the accident, radiation caused about eight hundred cases of thyroid cancer over the following decade. Scientists and doctors also suspected an increase in the rate of leukemia in the area. Whole communities in the area around Chernobyl were destroyed, and 130,000 people had to leave their homes because it was no longer safe to live there or grow crops on the contaminated soil.

The Chernobyl nuclear power plant (left) *spread radioactive materials over a large part of Eastern Europe when it melted down in 1986. This girl* (right) *got sick with leukemia shortly after the disaster, as is shown in the picture she holds of herself.*

 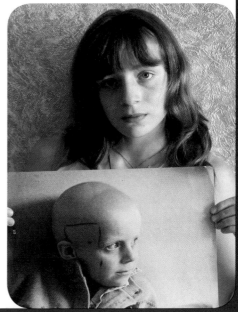

Nuclear power plants, such as this one in Gardanne, France, generate 16 percent of the world's electricity.

But nuclear energy has become an important alternative source of energy. Nuclear reactors are used to produce heat, boil water, and make steam. The steam is then used to drive a turbine—an engine that revolves when a substance such as steam passes through the blades of its wheel. The turbine produces electricity.

In 2006 nuclear power plants supplied about 16 percent of the world's electricity production. Except for Chernobyl, they have been extremely safe. Yet even if another deadly accident never occurs, there is another important concern. Nuclear power plants produce radioactive wastes, which have been piling up over the years.

Researchers have been looking for safe ways to get rid of radioactive waste. Ideas have included burying them in deep, stable underground caverns;

burning them so that only a dry powder remains; or combining them with cement to form solid concrete blocks. The most promising idea is vitrification. This involves sealing the wastes into a solid glass compound that will be stable for thousands of years. But still no one can agree on where to put the wastes. About the only site people agree on is NIMBY (not in my backyard).

Controlling Nuclear Energy

Scientists have been trying to find ways to control nuclear fusion reactions. But it is not easy to tame fusion reactions, since they require such extreme temperatures. It would not be wise to explode a fission bomb to start a fusion reaction, and the fission reaction in a nuclear reactor does not get hot enough, anyway. Researchers continue to look for answers.

Ultrasonic Clean

Extreme temperatures are needed to start a controlled thermonuclear fusion reaction. One possible approach uses high-frequency sound waves. These sound waves can be used to make tiny water bubbles pulsate. The bubbles expand, absorbing sound energy and then collapse violently, producing a shock wave that superheats the water and gives off a flash of light. Dentists use a milder version of the process, called cavitation, in instruments to clean teeth. Ultrasound makes tiny, pulsating water bubbles that blast away the plaque.

In 2006 the United States joined with six other partners (the European Union, Japan, China, India, the Republic of Korea, and the Russian Federation) to build a multibillion-dollar project. They plan to show that fusion power is possible and practical. The experimental power plant, in Cadarache in the south of France, is scheduled to be finished in 2016. The project is named ITER (from a Latin word meaning "the way"). It will produce about 500 megawatts of fusion power, using tiny amounts of deuterium and tritium (heavier forms of hydrogen).

In the reactor, a doughnut-shaped magnetic field will hold in the superhot gases. (At the high temperatures of a fusion reaction, the gas particles have so much kinetic energy that they would escape from a normal container, taking their energy with them and stopping the reaction.) An important goal of the ITER project is to design and test materials for the reactor walls. They must be able to withstand not only superhigh temperatures but also a stream of high-energy neutrons produced during fusion.

Fusion energy will not be completely free of pollution, since the neutrons can make reactor materials radioactive. But the amounts of radioactive waste would be hundreds of times less than for a fission reactor. And nuclear fusion would not release any carbon dioxide or sulfur or nitrogen compounds into the atmosphere.

Moreover, there would be no danger of a Chernobyl-like accident in a fusion reactor. Fusion

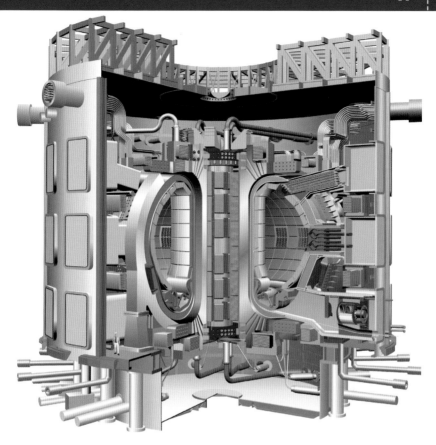

This computer illustration shows what the experimental fusion reactor being built by ITER will look like.

cannot turn into a runaway chain reaction. As soon as the hot gases came in contact with the walls of the reactor, they would cool down and the reaction would stop.

Fusion nuclear reactors seem to be a great idea for the future. They would be much safer than fission reactors and less costly. Their main fuels are cheap and readily available: deuterium can be obtained from seawater, and tritium can be made from lithium, a fairly common element. And fusion reactions do not produce nuclear wastes.

chapter eight

Alternative Energy Sources

Millions of years ago, very dense forests covered

most of the land on Earth. As the trees in the forests

died and decayed, they fell into swamps and became

buried in wet soil. Normally, soil microbes (microscopic

organisms) would feed on the dead trees, helping

the trees decay. But the wet soil did not hold enough

oxygen for these microbes to thrive. So the tree

remains did not decay.

The same thing happened in the large areas of shallow seas that covered much of Earth's surface millions of years ago. Billions of microscopic plantlike and animallike creatures lived in these waters. When these tiny organisms died, they fell to the bottom of the seafloor and became buried in the thick muck. The muck did not have enough oxygen to support living organisms. So the microscopic plants and animals did not decay.

Over a long period of time, the remains of the trees and the bodies of the tiny sea creatures were buried under layers of rock and soil. Eventually, under the huge pressure of the rocks above them, the remains of Earth's earlier life turned into coal, oil, and natural gas. These fossil fuels are highly valued in the modern world as important sources of energy.

In the twenty-first century, we use fossil fuels to heat homes, cook meals, drive our cars, run machines to give us electricity, and do many other kinds of work. But fossil fuels are a limited resource. The special conditions under which they were formed no longer exist. For this reason, researchers are working very hard to find alternative sources of energy. Fortunately, there are ways to generate energy using plentiful and renewable resources.

Left: *A coal miner walks through a mine shaft.* Right: *This offshore oil platform mines oil from under the ocean. Stores of oil, coal, and natural gas are limited.*

What Are Renewable Resources?

Renewable resources are resources that can be replaced fairly easily, in a reasonable amount of time. For example, solar energy is a renewable resource. We get a new supply from the Sun every day. The kinetic energy of flowing water is another renewable resource. So is the energy of blowing winds. Fossil fuels, however, are nonrenewable resources. Once they are used up, there will be no more to replace them.

Solar Power

Solar energy is a renewable resource that is growing in popularity. Solar panels on the roofs of buildings absorb some of the Sun's energy. This energy can be used to heat homes and produce electricity.

A device called a photovoltaic cell converts solar energy into electricity. The materials in a photovoltaic cell produce an electric current when light shines on them. If sunlight is used, the cell is called a solar cell. Large numbers of solar cells can be connected to form a solar battery. Low-powered solar batteries are used to power calculators, watches, and cameras. More powerful solar batteries provide electricity for space satellites and have been used in experimental airplanes and automobiles.

Power generated by photovoltaic cells is more expensive than power produced by burning fossil fuels. As the market for solar energy grows, however, and as more solar devices are made, the cost for each solar cell will drop. But why would people switch to solar energy, if it is still more expensive than oil, gas, or electric power sources? Many local regions and even whole nations are offering incentives for people to install solar devices. These include government loans, tax deductions, and rebates.

Germany has become the leading user of solar power in the world as a result of a national Electricity Feed Law. When rooftop solar panels create more electricity than a building needs, the excess is sent to the electric power grid supplying the local area. Homeowners get a credit on their electric bill for the

The owners of this house have added photovoltaic cells to their roof. These cells convert solar energy into electricity.

Light in the Desert

Earth's deserts get a lot of sunlight, and the Sun shines there as much as 350 days a year. Therefore, deserts are ideal sites for building huge solar energy plants. These power plants use concentrated solar power.

Thousands of curved mirrors turn through the day to keep focused on the Sun. They collect solar energy and send it to pipes containing a synthetic (artificial) oil. The hot sunlight, magnified by the mirrors, heats the oil as high as 735°F (390°C). The hot oil is pumped through a heat exchanger to produce steam, and the steam generates electricity in a steam turbine. (A steam turbine is a kind of engine in which

extra energy they supply. (In some cases, the credits are bigger than the bill!) Similar electricity feed-in laws and regulations are helping the growth of solar energy in countries such as Spain, Denmark, and Italy and in some parts of the United States and Canada.

The Power of Biomass

Biomass is the stored energy in plant material and animal wastes. It can be used as a power source by burning or decomposing these materials. The burning moving steam—very hot water vapor—under high pressure turns blades around a central rod. The rod is connected to a generator that produces electricity.)

A group of nine solar power plants was built in the Mojave Desert in California in the 1980s. They produce more than 350 megawatts of electricity. Pacific Gas and Electric (an energy company) is in the process of building the largest solar power plant in the world, Mojave Solar Park. When it is completed in 2011, it will cover about 6,000 acres (2,400 hectares, or 24 sq. km.) of desert land and produce 553 megawatts of electricity— enough to supply power to four hundred thousand homes.

process releases heat and light energy. Biomass is a renewable resource, because we can grow and raise more plants and animals.

Biomass is not a new energy source—its use dates from the discovery of fire. Early hunters and gatherers burned plants to warm themselves and cook their food. They also burned animal fat for their lanterns and torches and sometimes used animal bones for fires when wood was not available. In the twenty-first century, biomass is still the main energy source for more than half of the world's population.

Special containers called digesters are used to extract energy from biomass. In these containers, plant remains, such as straw, are mixed with animal wastes, such as cow manure. As the waste materials decompose, or rot, they make a natural gas called methane. Not just farm wastes but also household trash and industrial wastes will be sources of methane and other biomass fuels in the future.

Methane gas is formed naturally from decaying matter in stagnant ponds and marshes and in the gas that passes out of the intestines of people and animals. People tend to think of it as smelly, but actually methane is odorless. The smell comes from sulfur compounds produced along with it. Methane gas can be burned to heat houses, cook food, and produce electricity. It is more likely to be used in places with plenty of plant and animal wastes. Burning methane produces carbon dioxide, which can add to global warming. However, methane itself also contributes to global warming—twenty times as much as the same amount of carbon dioxide.

Biomass can also be used as a fuel source for automobiles. In Brazil, for instance, sugarcane crops are chopped down to make an alcohol called ethanol. Juice is extracted from plants and fermented to make alcohol, much like grape juice is turned into wine. Nearly all the new cars sold in Brazil can run on ethanol.

Most of the gasoline sold in the United States contains at least 10 percent ethanol. Many new cars can use gasoline that is mixed with larger amounts of ethanol. This ethanol is produced mainly from corn.

This man is unloading corn at an ethanol plant. The plant will process this corn and make it into ethanol, which will be used to fuel cars.

Some environmentalists say that ethanol made from food crops is not a good alternative energy source. It uses valuable land that could be growing food to feed hungry people. Moreover, it takes energy to grow the crops and convert them to ethanol. Ethanol fuel delivers only about 25 percent more energy than was used to produce it! Researchers are developing ways to produce ethanol from fast-growing crops that are not part of our food supply. These include grasses such as switchgrass and Miscanthus. Unlike corn, which must be replanted every year, these grasses are planted only once and grow new crops year after year. Studies sponsored by the U.S. Department of Agriculture have shown that ethanol made from switchgrass yields more than five times more energy than was used to produce it.

Researchers are exploring other nonfood crops, such as switchgrass (above), *as possible sources of biofuels.*

Fast-growing poplar trees are another promising energy source. A Central American shrub called *Jatropha* can grow on poor soils. It produces seeds whose oil can be converted to fuel for diesel trucks.

Geothermal Energy

Deep beneath Earth's surface lies a thick layer of hot gases and molten rock called magma. The temperature of this magma is about 3,000°F (1,650°C). Magma escapes from inside our planet's interior when volcanoes erupt and ooze out lava, releasing magma gases. Sometimes hot water or steam shoots out from tiny cracks in the rock and creates hot springs. Animals, such as the Florida

manatee, retreat to these hot springs during seasonal
migration. The manatees spend the summer in the coastal
waters off North and South Carolina and then swim down
to Georgia and Florida for the winter. They gather around
natural hot springs and the warm-water outlets of electric
power plants. Hot springs were used by ancient Romans to
warm their baths, and they are used in modern Iceland to heat
buildings.

Energy that comes from inside Earth is called geothermal
energy. It is a naturally occurring energy source, and the supply
is practically limitless. Hot springs do not occur everywhere.
But geothermal energy can be tapped by drilling down to
the hot rocks, especially in places like Japan, the Philippines,
California, and the west coast of South America, where

*This power plant on the Blue Lagoon near Reykjavik, Iceland, runs on
geothermal energy.*

magma is closer to the surface. Water sent down into the holes is superheated. It turns into steam as it rises back up to the surface. The steam can then be used to turn the turbines that produce electricity.

But it's not always necessary to drill into the depths of the planet to use geothermal power. On a small scale, we can get usable heat from the soil. For example, devices called heat pumps can move heat from about 50 feet (15 m) below the surface to heat a house in the winter or to air-condition it in the summer. These pumps can work for any house, anywhere in the world.

One problem is that geothermal power plants may give off sulfur compounds. These compounds not only smell like rotten eggs but contribute to acid rain that can destroy forests and damage buildings. Engineers are looking for ways to filter out the sulfur gases.

Geothermal power is one of the fastest-growing alternative energy sources. In the period from 2000 to 2005, the number of geothermal power plants in the world increased about 24 percent *each year*. Geothermal power plants can work twenty-four hours a day, all year long, in all weather. In some areas, the electricity they produce is just as cheap as the power made with fossil fuels, and it is more dependable. We don't need to worry about running out of this power source, either. The world's reserves of geothermal energy are about fifteen thousand times as great as all our oil and gas reserves.

Wind Power

Wind power is actually a form of solar energy at work.
Wind is created as a result of convection. You may remember
that heated air rises and is replaced by cooler air, setting up
convection currents. The Sun warms the air at the equator and
causes the heated air to rise. At the same time, colder air from
the polar regions moves in to replace the heated air. These air
movements, combined with Earth's rotation, create wind.

Windmills, or wind turbines, tap into the wind's energy.
Have you ever blown on the sails of a pinwheel and watched
them fly around in a circle? That is what a wind turbine looks

*Wind turbines on a wind farm like this one change wind energy into
electricity.*

like. Wind moves the sails of the wind turbine, which, like a steam turbine, then produces electricity. Some wind turbines can make enough electricity to light twenty thousand lightbulbs at once.

However, wind turbines make electricity only when the wind blows. And the hours of the day when that happens do not usually match the daytime peak hours of energy demand by homes and businesses. Researchers are developing better energy storage devices, to build up power reserves when the wind is blowing.

During the five years from 2001 to 2006, the wind industry grew an average of 17 percent a year, all over the world. The United States is the world leader in wind power, but countries in Europe built more than half of all the new systems. Wind power is also growing rapidly in India and China.

Waterpower

Waterpower is another ancient energy source that holds promise for the future. Oceanic waves crashing against rocks and waterfalls cascading downward hold great amounts of energy. One way to use this power is through waterwheels. The movement of water is used to drive turbines, which produce electricity. Hydroelectricity power dams (*hydro* means "water") use the force of falling water to turn turbines.

In waterfalls and dams, potential energy is changed to kinetic energy as water moves from

Grand Coulee Dam in the state of Washington is the largest hydropower producer in the United States. It is on the Columbia River.

higher places to lower ones. The natural tides that flow through the seas and oceans are driven by a different force: the pull of the Moon's gravity. The rise and fall of the tides make wavelike movements in the water. The power of waves can be used to run turbines.

In 1966 France opened a power plant that used tidal power. Great Britain has become the world leader in wave and tidal energy development. In the United States, a tidal power plant is operating in Passamaquoddy Bay, between Maine and Canada. Another one is being built for the naval base in Hawaii. Studies of tidal currents under way in California, Oregon, Washington, and New Jersey may lead to the building of new tidal power plants there.

One problem with hydropower is that it can change the ecology (relations between organisms and their environment) of the region. It may affect the fish and other organisms living in the coastal waters. A tidal power plant may change the water temperature and the amount of nutrients and sediment (rocks, sand, or dirt) in the water. It alters the network of rivers and streams that carry water draining from the land and connect with the coastal ocean waters. The animals and plants of a particular place are used to the conditions there. If these conditions change, some kinds of water life may not be able to adapt. Studies

This tidal power plant is in Nova Scotia, Canada. It uses the tides to generate electricity.

Energy

These are turbines inside the tidal power station in Brittany, France. The changing tides turn the turbines that generate electricity.

of the French tidal power plant in 1995, however, showed that after thirty years of operation, the coastal waters were still home to a rich and varied assortment of aquatic wildlife. There seemed to be no great harmful changes.

chapter nine

A Green Future?

For years many scientists have been warning the public about global warming—a significant rise in the average temperature of the planet. They believe that the burning of fuels has been increasing the amount of carbon dioxide and other heat-trapping gases in the atmosphere. These heat-trapping gases work kind of like an extra blanket on your bed. The extra carbon dioxide blanket has been making Earth warmer just like your extra blanket makes you warmer.

Warmer temperatures mean serious problems for our planet. Over the next hundred years, global warming could increase Earth's average temperature by a few degrees. This does not sound like much, but it would be enough to melt much of the ice and snow in the polar regions. The melted ice would raise the sea level and flood many of the world's coastal areas, such as New York City and the whole state of Florida. Global warming would also change the climate of our planet.

Greenhouse Planet

Earth's atmosphere acts very much like the glass of a greenhouse. Like the glass roof and walls of a greenhouse, our atmosphere traps heat from sunlight. The greenhouse effect has been keeping Earth comfortably warm and, in fact, has made life possible on our planet. Over the last century or two, however, human activities have been producing large amounts of heat-trapping gases. The increase in these "greenhouse gases" in the atmosphere may make our planet too hot to suit the needs of the animals and plants that live on Earth.

The increase in heat-trapping gases over the last century allows less of the Sun's radiation to escape back into space, resulting in a warmer planet.

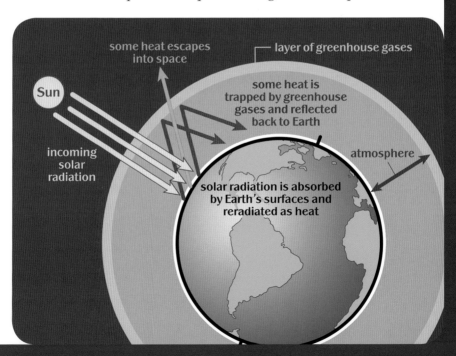

Lands that are too cold most of the year to grow food crops might become important food suppliers for the world. Much of the United States, Europe, and Asia would become tropical—hot for most of the year. These parts of the world might no longer have four seasons each year. Winters would be shorter and warmer or disappear entirely. Summers would be longer and hotter. Meanwhile, the number of severe storms would increase.

Scientists have pointed out that we are already seeing the beginnings of these drastic changes in our weather and climate. They have been warning that if we do not change our ways, we may reach a point where we may no longer be able to stop the warming trend.

For the most part, people have ignored these warnings. It wasn't until 2006 that global warming gained widespread, global attention with the documentary film, *An Inconvenient Truth*. The film, featuring former U.S. vice president Al Gore, won an Oscar. Gore discusses scientific evidence for global warming and the role that humans play in adding to the warming of the planet. Global warming, he insists, has already had serious effects on our weather and climate. If we do not reduce the

Did You Know?
Most greenhouse gases remain in the atmosphere for about a hundred years or more. So efforts to reduce greenhouse emissions will not have noticeable results for a long time.

billions of tons of carbon dioxide we produce every year, the effects could be disastrous. The film's message was loud and clear—we need cleaner alternative energy sources and we need to conserve energy for our future generations.

Going Green

An Inconvenient Truth made the general public think. Soon many people became enthusiastic about going green—that is, conserving energy and reducing

Al Gore (left) *and Davis Guggenheim, the director of* An Inconvenient Truth, *pose with their Oscar following the 2007 Academy Awards.*

pollution to help the environment. "Green" has become the new buzzword—a synonym for environmentally friendly. People can buy products made from recycled materials or renewable resources. For example, people can buy products made from recyclable paper instead of from plastics. Or they can buy clothing made of cotton or wool instead of synthetic materials made from petroleum.

Not just individuals are going green these days. Since 2000, for example, New York City has been switching its diesel-fueled buses to a cleaner-burning fuel with 90 percent less sulfur. Effective filters have also helped to reduce polluting emissions from the diesel buses. By the end of 2007, more than five hundred new buses had hybrid engines, burning much less fossil fuel. Other cities across the United States are also replacing their bus fleets with diesel-electric hybrids. The new buses cost more than the old diesel buses, but they are quieter, more efficient, and much kinder to the environment. Many communities are also installing pollution-trapping filters on their diesel school buses.

Some large companies are taking steps to cut down pollution from industrial and agricultural

Many cities are switching to diesel-electric hybrid buses (below) *to save money and help protect the environment.*

Energy

machines. Wal-Mart, for example, has begun using forklifts, which are used to move heavy loads, that run on fuel cells in its big distribution centers. Older forklifts were powered by less efficient and more polluting diesel engines.

The idea of going green and saving energy is actually nothing new. An earlier wave of enthusiasm for saving energy occurred in the 1970s. It was sparked by an energy crisis due to a dramatic increase in the price of oil. A group of Middle Eastern oil-producing nations had joined to form an organization called the Organization of Petroleum Exporting Countries (OPEC). OPEC set (and still sets) the price of oil and strict limits on the amount of oil sold. Consumers all around the world waited in line for gasoline. Fuel oil bills doubled and tripled and doubled again.

Gradually, people realized that they had developed energy-wasting habits. They were driving cars when they could walk and were setting their thermostats too high in the winter and too low in the summer. All over the world, people began to think more about ways to conserve energy. They began insulating houses better so heat would not be lost to the outside and turning off lights when leaving a room.

The OPEC oil crisis proved to be temporary. As oil prices eventually plunged, people forgot about the importance of conserving energy. In fact, gas-guzzling sport-utility vehicles (SUVs) became popular in the 1990s, and the energy crisis seemed like a distant memory. These days, however, energy has once again become a hot topic. The price of oil is again very high, and we know that our reserves of oil and other fossil fuels are limited. We need to conserve energy to make them last as long as possible. We also need to put more effort into developing alternative, renewable energy sources to replace them. These new energy sources should also be "clean" to avoid producing harmful pollution and adding to the greenhouse gases that lead to global warming.

What You Can Do

Many governments around the world are trying to work out a suitable energy plan. You and your family can also do many things to conserve energy and help the environment. They include the following:

- Cut down on your use of electricity. Turn off the lights, the computer, or the television when you are not using them.
- Buy energy-efficient machines and appliances. Look for the Energy Star label. That means the product is designed to save energy.
- Recycle items such as newspapers, aluminum cans, corrugated cardboard, and plastics instead of throwing them away.
- Avoid gas-guzzling family cars. Instead, consider energy-efficient cars that don't use a lot of gasoline to drive long distances. Hybrid cars, which get great gas mileage on a limited amount of gasoline, are growing in popularity.
- Try walking, riding a bike, or taking the bus instead of having someone drive you to places that are not far, such as the corner store or your friend's house down the street.

Right: *Recycling everyday items such as newspapers, cans, and bottles is an easy way to help the environment.* **Below:** *Driving a hybrid car helps save energy and reduces fuel costs.*

- Make sure your home is energy efficient. Walls and ceilings should be insulated. Use caulk or weather stripping around windows and doorways. Your power company can do an energy audit. Someone comes to your house and points out where energy might be escaping. You use more fuel when your house is not energy efficient.
- Don't let the water faucet run too long when washing your hands in the bathroom at home, school, the mall, restaurant, or any other place. (Wasting water means wasting electricity.)
- Take shorter showers. You'll use less hot water. Water heaters make up almost 25 percent of your home's energy use.
- Turn off battery-operated toys or games when you are done with them. The batteries will last longer, so you won't have to replace them too often.

Whenever you save energy, or use it more efficiently, you reduce the need for gasoline, oil, coal, and natural gas. That means you will be burning fewer fossil fuels, which in turn means less carbon dioxide in the atmosphere. In addition, alternative energy sources, such as solar energy, wind energy, and geothermal energy, may someday become the standard energy sources of everyday life. Not only would these energy sources help reduce air pollution even further, but they would also give us an endless supply of energy. All these solutions, including various energy-saving tips and even planting trees, are not only good for you and your family, they are also good for our planet.

Glossary

alpha particle: a type of radiation consisting of a helium nucleus (two protons and two neutrons)

alternating current (AC): current electricity in which electrons move in one direction and then change and flow in the opposite direction

amplitude: the height of a wave

anode: a positively charged electrode; negatively charged particles and electrons move toward it

atomic number: the number of protons in the nucleus of an atom of a particular element

atoms: tiny particles that are the building blocks of chemical elements

ATP (adenosine triphosphate): a chemical compound that can store large amounts of energy and release them readily

battery: an energy-storage device that releases electricity upon demand

beta particle: a type of radiation consisting of an electron or a positron (a rare kind of electron with a positive electrical charge)

biomass: plant material and animal wastes used to generate power

cathode: a negatively charged electrode; it releases electrons, and positively charged particles move toward it

cavitation: the production of tiny water bubbles by blasts of ultrasound

chain reaction: a series of reactions in which one reaction causes the next to occur

chemical energy: energy stored in the bonds that hold atoms together in molecules

chlorophyll: the green pigment in plant cells that gathers light energy

chloroplasts: structures in plant cells in which photosynthesis occurs

circuit: the path along which current electricity flows

compass: a device for navigation in which a free-moving iron needle always points to Earth's magnetic north pole

compound: a substance formed by chemical joining of atoms into molecules

compression waves: sound waves that travel by squeezing the molecules in the medium through which they move

condensation: a change of state of matter from liquid to solid or gas to liquid

conduction: the direct transfer of heat through a substance

conductor: a substance that can carry electricity from one place to another

control rods: neutron-absorbing rods placed among the uranium rods in a nuclear reactor to keep the reaction controlled

convection: the transfer of heat by the movement of a heated substance

convection currents: flows of a moving substance that transfer heat

critical mass: the smallest amount of uranium that will keep a chain reaction going

current electricity: the energy produced by moving electrons or ions

decay: the breakdown of an unstable atom into smaller particles

deuterium: a form of hydrogen containing one proton and one neutron in the nucleus of each atom; also called heavy hydrogen

digester: a container used to convert biomass to methane

direct current (DC): current electricity that flows in only one direction

domain: a cluster of atoms in a magnetizable metal such as iron

echolocation: a method used by bats, dolphins, and other animals to detect objects by sending out high-pitched sounds that bounce off the object and come back to the animal's ears

electrical energy: energy involving the movement of charged particles (electrons or ions)

electric field: the space around a charged particle that is affected by the charge

electricity: a property of matter caused by the presence and motion of electrons or ions; electric current or power

electrode: a device through which electric current passes into or out of a conducting substance

electromagnet: a coil of wire wrapped around an iron bar that produces a strong magnetic field when electric current flows through it

electromagnetic field (EMF): the space around a wire through which electric current flows, producing magnetic effects

electromagnetic induction: the production of electric current when a magnet is moved through a closed coil of wire

electromagnetic radiation: waves consisting of electrical and magnetic fields traveling together

electromagnetic spectrum: the whole range of energy, from radio waves to gamma rays

electron: a negatively charged particle that moves around the nucleus of an atom and may move freely through an electrical conductor

elements: the simplest chemical substances, consisting of atoms of all the same kind

energy: the capacity to do work

entropy: the state of disorder of a system; the amount of energy that has been converted to unusable forms and is wasted

evaporation: a change of state of matter from liquid to gas

fission fragments: the particles into which the nucleus of an atom splits during nuclear fission

fossil fuels: coal, oil, and gas; produced by the preservation of plant and animal remains under high-pressure conditions

frequency: the number of waves that pass a given point in a certain time

fuel cell: a battery that changes chemical energy directly to current electricity

gamma radiation: shortwave, high-energy radiation produced in transformations inside the nuclei of atoms

gamma rays: high-energy packets of electromagnetic energy

geothermal energy: energy derived from the hot matter inside Earth

global warming: a significant rise in the average temperature throughout the world

gravitational energy: energy associated with the force of attraction between two objects of matter

greenhouse effect: a warming of Earth due to atmospheric gases such as carbon dioxide, which trap heat like the glass in a greenhouse

half-life: the amount of time it takes for half the atoms of a radioisotope to decay into another element or isotope

heat energy: energy involving the movement of molecules

hydrogen bomb: an explosive device in which an atomic fission bomb is used to produce enough heat for a fusion reaction to take place

infrared radiation: heat radiation that is just beyond the long-wave end of the visible spectrum

insulation: a layer of non-heat-conducting material used to control the transfer of heat energy

insulator: a substance that cannot conduct electricity

intensity: the amount of energy carried by sound waves; the loudness of a sound

internal energy: the kinetic energy of substances due to moving particles

ion: an electrically charged particle formed from an atom or molecule that has lost or gained one or more electrons

isotopes: forms of an element with the same atomic number but different mass numbers

kinetic energy: energy of motion

laser: a device that uses excited atoms to generate a very strong, tightly focused beam of light of a single wavelength, in which all the photons move in step with the others

light energy: energy involving the movement of light particles

magma: the molten rock and hot gases beneath Earth's surface

magnetic field: the area surrounding a pole of a magnet, which exerts attractive or repulsive forces on objects

magnetism: energy associated with electricity and involving an attraction to objects made of iron, nickel, or cobalt

mass number: the total number of protons and neutrons in the nucleus of an atom; also called atomic weight

matter: anything that has a definite amount of mass and takes up space

mechanical energy: energy involving the movement of machine parts

methane: a natural gas formed from decaying matter

microwaves: low-energy radiation, with the second-longest wavelength in the electromagnetic spectrum

mitochondria: cell structures in which respiration occurs

molecules: the building blocks of matter, consisting of atoms joined by chemical bonds

neutron: a particle with no electrical charge that is found in the nucleus of an atom

nuclear energy: energy stored within the nuclei of atoms

nuclear fission: the splitting of the nucleus of a heavy atom into two or more large parts

nuclear force: the strong binding force that holds together the protons and neutrons in an atomic nucleus

nuclear fusion: a nuclear reaction in which two atomic nuclei join to form the nucleus of a different element

nuclear reaction: the breaking apart or joining together of atomic nuclei

OPEC: an organization of Middle Eastern oil-producing countries that sets limits on oil production and exports

orbital: the path traveled by an electron around the nucleus of an atom

photon: a packet of light energy; a light particle

photosynthesis: a process in which living organisms use sunlight (solar) energy to make carbohydrates from carbon dioxide and water, producing oxygen as a by-product

photovoltaic cell: a device that converts solar energy to electricity; also called a solar cell

pitch: how high or low a sound seems to a listener; it is determined by the sound frequency

poles: the regions of a magnet where its magnetic effects are the strongest

potential energy: stored energy that has the potential to do work

prism: an angled piece of glass that splits light into the spectrum of colors

proton: a positively charged particle found in the nucleus of an atom

radiant energy: energy transmitted in a wave of motion; also a synonym for light

radiation: the movement of heat energy through empty space; also forms of energy in the electromagnetic spectrum

radiation sickness: illness due to the damaging effects of radiation on the body

radioactive decay (radioactivity): the spontaneous breakdown of an unstable atomic nucleus, releasing radiation

radioisotope: an unstable form of an element that gives off radiation when it breaks down

radio waves: long-wave electromagnetic radiation used to carry information in radio and television broadcasts

reflection: the bouncing of light rays back toward their origin

refraction: the bending of light rays when they pass through the boundary between two different substances

respiration: a process in living cells in which carbohydrates and other organic carbon compounds react with oxygen, releasing energy and producing carbon dioxide as a waste product

solar energy: energy from the Sun that is converted to heat or electrical energy

spectrum: the band of colors produced by the separation of light of different wavelengths

static electricity: the energy of electric charges at rest

temperature: a measure of the heat in a substance

thermodynamics: the branch of physics that studies the relationships between heat and other forms of energy and conversions of one to another

thermonuclear fusion reaction: a nuclear reaction in which extremely high temperatures are used to produce fusion of atomic nuclei

tidal power: use of the energy of moving water produced by the gravitational pull of the Moon

tritium: form of hydrogen whose nuclei contain one proton and two neutrons

turbine: an engine that revolves when a substance, such as steam, water, or wind, passes through the blades of its wheel

ultrasound: sound energy with a higher frequency that humans can hear

ultraviolet radiation: black light, just beyond the shortwave end of the visible spectrum

vibration: back-and-forth movement; for example, that of a plucked guitar

visible light: the part of the electromagnetic spectrum that humans can see

wavelength: the distance between the top of one wave and the top of the next

work: movement of an object of production of a change in the state of matter

X-rays: shortwave, high-energy radiation; like visible light, X-rays can trigger chemical reactions in the coating of film, producing an image

Bibliography

Almeida, Carla. "Sugarcane Ethanol: Brazil's Biofuel Success." *Science and Development Network*. January 3, 2008. http://www.enn.com/ecosystems/article/28580 (January 3, 2008).

Bioenergy Feedstock Development Program, Oak Ridge National Laboratory. "Biofuels from Switchgrass: Greener Energy Pastures." *BFIN*. N.d. http://bioenergy.ornl.gov/papers/misc/switgrs.html (January 2, 2008).

Brain, Marshall. "How CDs Work." *How Stuff Works*. 1998–2008. http://electronics.howstuffworks.com/cd.htm (February 20, 2008).

Cameron, Alasdair. "Growth on All Fronts: The BTM Wind Market Update." *Renewable Energy World*. July 2007. http://www.renewable-energy-world.com/articles/article_display.cfm?ARTICLE_ID=305265&p=121 (January 2, 2008).

Clynes, Tom. "The Energy Fix: 10 Steps to End America's Fossil Fuel Addiction." *Popular Science*, July 2006, 47–61.

Eco-Pros. "Renewable and Nonrenewable Resources." *Eco-Pros: Environmental Education on the Web*. May 20, 2006. http://www.eco-pros.com/renewableresources.htm (December 31, 2007).

Energy Information Administration. "Ethanol Timeline." *Energy Kid's Page, Department of Energy*. November 2005. http://www.eia.doe.gov/kids/history/timelines/ethanol.html (January 3, 2008).

Scholastic Books. *Exploring Energy*. New York: Scholastic, 1995.

Gutnik, Martin J., and Natalie Browne-Gutnik. *The Energy Question: Thinking about Tomorrow*. Hillside, NJ: Enslow, 1993.

Harvey, Jonathan. "A Versatile Solution? Growing Miscanthus for Bioenergy." *Renewable Energy World*. January 2007. http://www.renewable-energy-world.com/articles/article_display.cfm?ARTICLE_ID=284688&p=121 (January 3, 2008).

IEA. "Key World Energy Statistics 2007." *International Energy Agency*. 2007. http://www.iea.org/Textbase/publications/free_new_Desc.asp?PUBS_ID=1199 (January 10, 2008).

Johnston, Tom. *Science in Action: Electricity Turns the World On!* Milwaukee: Gareth Stevens, 1988.

Jones, Jackie, and Alasdair Cameron. "Solar Movement: How Solar Heat Is Producing Power on Both Sides of the Atlantic." *Renewable Energy World.* July 2007. http://www .renewable-energy-world.com/articles/article_display .cfm?ARTICLE_ID=305276&p=121 (January 2, 2008).

Kent, Amanda, and Alan Ward. *Introduction to Physics.* London: Usborne, 1983.

Layton, Julia, and Karim Nice. "How Hybrid Cars Work." *How Stuff Works.* July 20, 2000. http://auto.howstuffworks.com/ hybrid-car.htm (January 2, 2008).

NEVC. "E85: Frequently Asked Questions." *National Ethanol Vehicle Coalition.* N.d. http://www.e85fuel.com/e85101/ questions.php (January 3, 2008).

Nice, Karim, and Jonathan Strickland. "How Fuel Cells Work." *How Stuff Works.* September 18, 2000. http://auto .howstuffworks.com/fuel-cell.htm (January 2, 2008).

Pandya, C. G. "Tidal Energy Update." *Earthtoys—The Renewable Energy Magazine.* April 2006. http://www.earthtoys.com/ emagazine.php?issue_number=06.04.01&article=tidal (January 8, 2008).

Parker, Steve. *Eyewitness Science: Electricity.* New York: Dorling Kindersley, 1992.

PPPL. "ITER and the Promise of Fusion Energy." *Princeton Plasma Physics Laboratory.* February 2006. http://www.pppl .gov/projects/pics/ITER4pg.pdf (January 7, 2008).

Suplee, Curt. "No Greater Cancer Risk Is Found in Children Living Near Power Lines: Federal Study Tries to Shed Light on High-Voltage Debate." *Washington Post,* July 3, 1997, A1.

U.S. Department of Energy. "The History of Solar." *Energy Efficiency and Renewable Energy.* October 24, 2006. http:// www1.eere.energy.gov/solar/pdfs/solar_timeline.pdf (January 7, 2008).

Veggeberg, Scott. "New Uses Found for Electricity in Bone Disease." *Nutrition Health Review*, Spring 1990. 2004. http://findarticles.com/p/articles/mi_m0876/is_n54/ai_9252119 (December 24, 2007).

Vogt, Gregory. *Electricity and Magnetism*. New York: Franklin Watts, 1985.

Wald, Matthew L. "Hybrid Cars Burning Gas in the Drive for Power." *New York Times*. July 17, 2005. http://www.nytimes.com/2005/07/17/automobiles/17hybrid.html (December 24, 2007).

Wechsler, Matthew. "How Lasers Work." *How Stuff Works*. April 1, 2000. http://science.howstuffworks.com/laser.htm (March 31, 2008).

Wellington, Jerry. *The Super Science Book of Energy*. New York: Thomson Learning, 1994.

Whalley, Margaret. *Interfact: Electricity and Magnetism*. Chicago: World Book, 1997 (includes an interactive CD-ROM).

For Further Information

Books

DK Publishing. *Energy*. New York: DK Children, 2007.

Fairly, Peter. *Electricity and Magnetism*. Minneapolis: Twenty-First Century Books, 2008.

Fleisher, Paul. *Matter and Energy*. Minneapolis: Twenty-First Century Books, 2002.

Fridell, Ron. *Earth-Friendly Energy*. Minneapolis: Lerner Publications Company, 2009.

Jefferis, David. *Green Power: Eco-Energy Without Pollution*. New York: Crabtree Publishing Company, 2006.

Johnson, Rebecca L. *Understanding Global Warming*. Minneapolis: Lerner Publications Company, 2009.

———. *Investigating Climate Change*. Minneapolis: Twenty-First Century Books, 2009.

Landau, Elaine. *The History of Energy*. Minneapolis: Lerner Publications Company, 2006.

Meiani, Antonella. *Magnetism*. Minneapolis: Lerner Publications Company, 2003.

Parker, Steve. *The Science of Electricity & Magnetism: Projects and Experiments with Electricity and Magnets*. Chicago: Heinemann Library, 2005.

Saunders, Nigel, and Steven Chapman. *Renewable Energy*. Chicago: Raintree, 2005.

VanCleave, Janice. *Janice VanCleave's Energy for Every Kid: Easy Activities That Make Learning Science Fun*. San Francisco: Jossey-Bass, 2005.

Walker, Niki. *Biomass: Fueling Change*. New York: Crabtree Publishing Company, 2006.

———. *Generating Wind Power*. New York: Crabtree Publishing Company, 2006.

————. *Harnessing Power from the Sun*. New York: Crabtree Publishing Company, 2006.

————. *Hydrogen: Running on Water*. New York: Crabtree Publishing Company, 2006.

Websites

Alliant Energy Kids: Making Energy Fun and Safe
http://www.powerhousekids.com/stellent2/groups/public/documents/pub/phk_001537.hcsp
Through interactive lessons and activities, kids can learn about electricity and natural gas, how to use them safely, and ways to conserve energy.

Atomic Energy of Canada Limited: Kids' Zone
http://www.aecl.ca/kidszone/atomicenergy/
A fun, colorful website with lots of information on energy in kid-friendly language. It also has plenty of fun facts, as well as games and activities.

Energy: A Guide for Kids by Tiki the Penguin
http://tiki.oneworld.net/energy/energy.html
Tiki the penguin makes learning about energy fun as you follow the penguin in colorful cartoons, accompanied by a down-to-earth discussion of energy basics, as well as nonrenewable energy sources, pollution, and their effects on our planet. The site also talks about renewable energy sources and ways people can help conserve energy.

Energy Information Administration (EIA): Energy Kid's Page
http://www.eia.doe.gov/kids/
This website contains information on nonrenewable and renewable energy sources, energy-saving tips, as well as fun games and activities about energy.

Kids Konnect: Electricity
http://www.kidskonnect.com/content/view/72/27/
This is a gateway site, with links to lots of sites about electricity. Click on the links to find interactive lessons, experiments, games, and activities, as well as information on safety with electricity.

Kids Saving Energy

http://www.eere.energy.gov/kids/

Sponsored by the U.S. Department of Energy, this kid-friendly site contains information on renewable energy, lots of helpful energy-saving tips for your home, and games and activities. The Energy Quest "Movieroom" has downloadable videos and animated films on various energy-related topics.

Solar Energy International: Renewable Energy for a Sustainable Future—Kid's Info

http://www.solarenergy.org/resources/youngkids.html

In a question-and-answer format, this website discusses various aspects of solar energy, as well as its future as a promising alternative energy source.

Index

Photo Acknowledgments

The images in this book are used with the permission of: Milch & Markt Informationsbüro, www.milch-markt.de , p. 7 (left); © Shannon Fagan/Taxi/Getty Images, p. 7 (right); © Barry Rosenthal/Taxi/Getty Images, p. 8; © Hulton Archive/ Getty Images, p. 13; © David Frazier/Stone/Getty Images, p. 17; © Jeffrey Coolidge/ The Image Bank//Getty Images, p. 19 (left); © Dr. Marli Miller/Visuals Unlimited, p. 19 (right); © Stillfx/Dreamstime.com, p. 21; © UPI/drr.net, p. 24; © Scientifica/ Visuals Unlimited, p. 27; © Leonard Lessin/Peter Arnold, Inc., p. 29; © Phil Degginger/Alamy, p. 30; © iStockphoto.com/Satu Knape, p. 39; © Tim Flach/ Riser/Getty Images, p. 43 (top); © U. Bellhaeuser/ScienceFoto/Getty Images, p. 45; © iStockphoto.com/Martin McCarthy, p. 52; © Johnny Lye/Fotolia.com, p. 53 (left); © Nana Twumasi/Independent Picture Service, p. 53(right); © Jason Hindley/ Photonica/Getty Images, p. 56 (left); © David Trood/The Image Bank/Getty Images, p. 56 (right); © Reza Estakhrian/Taxi/Getty Images, p. 57; The Illustrated London News, p. 58; © BananaStock/Hotshoe/Photoshot, p. 59; © Paul Chesley/National Geographic/Getty Images, p. 60; © iStockphoto.com/Robert Kohlhuber, p. 63; © iStockphoto.com/Martin Fischer, p. 65; © Roger Tully/The Medical File/Peter Arnold, Inc., p. 69; National Archives, p. 73; © Arthur Hill/Visuals Unlimited, p. 74; Princeton University Library, p. 75; © Hans Neleman/Stone/Getty Images, p. 77; © PhotoXpress/ZUMA Press, pp. 81 (both); © Photodisc/Getty Images, pp. 82, 87 (right); courtesy of ITER, p. 85; © Tyler Stableford/Stone/Getty Images, p. 87 (left); © iStockphoto.com/Richard Schmidt-Zuper, p. 89; AP Photo/Charlie Neibergall, p. 93; © Paul Debois/Gap Photo/Visuals Unlimited, p. 94; © Picturegarden/ Photonica/Getty Images, p. 95; © iStockphoto.com/Stephen Strathdee, p. 97; © iStockphoto.com/Eric Foltz , p. 99; © Stephen Saks Photography/Alamy, p. 100; © Chris Howes/Wild Places Photography/Alamy, p. 101; AP Photo/Kevork Djansezian, p. 105; © Todd Strand/Independent Picture Service, pp. 106, 109 (top); © Julie Caruso/Independent Picture Service, p. 109 (bottom); Illustrations by: © Bill Hauser/Independent Picture Service, p. 5; © Laura Westlund/Independent Picture Service, pp. 15, 20, 33, 41, 42, 45 (bottom), 47, 67, 103.

Front Cover: © iStockphoto.com/Elena Elisseeva

About the Authors

Dr. Alvin Silverstein is a former professor of biology and director of the physician assistant program at the College of Staten Island of the City University of New York. Virginia B. Silverstein is a translator of Russian scientific literature.

The Silversteins' collaboration began with a biochemical research project at the University of Pennsylvania. Since then they have produced six children and more than two hundred published books that have received high acclaim for their clear, timely, and authoritative coverage of science and health topics.

Laura Silverstein Nunn, a graduate of Kean College, began helping with the research for her parents' books while she was in high school. Since joining the writing team, she has coauthored more than eighty books.